CW01649996

GOOD FOOD CLUB GUIDE

EDITED BY NICK JONES

The Essex Good Food Club Guide is published by The Essex Good Food Club.
The Essex Good Food Club is a county member of The Good Food Club (GB). PO Box 131, Berkhamsted, Herts, HP4 3XT

Typographic design by Judy Irving

A catalogue for this book is available from The British Library.

ISBN 0-9530385-4-8

The contents of this publication are believed correct at the time of printing. Nevertheless the Publishers cannot be held responsible for any errors or omissions or for changes relating to any details given in this Guide, including prices, ownership or quality. The Publishers would like to make it clear that they in no way have any ownership or other such connections with any of the establishments mentioned in this Guide.

Assessments of the establishments in this Guide are based on the experience(s) of Club correspondents on the occasion of their visit(s) and therefore the descriptions given in this Guide may contain an element of subjective opinion which may not dictate a reader's experience on another occasion.

The Essex Good Food Club would like to receive readers comments on any establishment either featured, or not featured in the Guide. We can then take your comments into account when preparing future editions. Please send your correspondence or a report form (report forms are included at the rear of this Guide) to:
The Editor, The Essex Good Food Club Guide c/o TheGood Food Club (GB), PO Box 131, Berkhamsted, Herts, HP4 3XT. Alternatively, e-mail us @thegoodfoodclub@hotmail.com

Advertisements appearing in this Guide are by invitation of The Essex Good Food Club. They are accepted after the establishments have been selected to appear in the Guide. Revenue generated from advertising and sponsorship, enables the Guide to be priced at a realistic level. The Essex Good Food Club would like to thank all advertisers and sponsors for their support.

Special thanks to Trevor, Chris and Jason for the design of this guide.

Front Cover Photo: Marygreen Manor, Brentwood

Printed and bound in the UK by Bartham Press Ltd, Luton, Beds.

Contents

INTRODUCTION

Firstly, thank you for choosing this guide.

The Essex Good Food Club Guide has been compiled to provide readers with a cross section of good places to eat. It is the intention of the guide to provide details of establishments which cater for all tastes, styles, budgets and occasions. By using this Guide, readers can discover restaurants (formal and informal), pubs, cafés, wine bars and bistros and we thank the proprietors and managers for providing the factual information, including opening times, average prices and non-smoking arrangements. In addition, we have included a brief description of each establishment. There is no use of symbols or ratings, we just set the scene and allow you to make an informed choice.

In most instances, the average price quoted is for a three course for two, inclusive of a bottle of house wine, coffee and service. However, it is suggested that readers check when making a reservation that prices and other details quoted meet their requirements, as these are often subject to change. To assist readers, the entries in this guide have been placed in cuisine order, with each establishment being listed alphabetically. Establishments that are not 'cuisine specific' are listed in the 'Other/Speciality' category. Purchasers of this guide are able to join the Essex Good Food Club free of charge. For more details, see our 'Join the Club' advertisment on page 112.

Finally, we hope that The Essex Good Food Club Guide will provide you with the basis for many intimate dinners, special occasions, business lunches, or just an informal snack.

Don't forget that we rely on readers comments to enable us to produce future editions and we are always pleased to receive your comments, be them praise, recommendations or criticism (report forms are provided at the rear of the Guide). Please mark your envelopes for the attention of 'The Editor', The Essex Good Food Club Guide. Our address is The Essex Good Food Club, c/o The Good Food Club (GB), PO Box 131, Berkhamsted, Herts, HP4 3XT.

Alternatively e-mail your comments to thegoodfoodclub@hotmail.com

At the time of publishing this guide, our new website was under construction. For more information on the club and its activities, see www.thegoodfoodclub.co.uk

We look forward to hearing from you!!

In the meantime - happy eating...

THE
ESSEX
GOOD FOOD
CLUB GUIDE

A Word About Our Sponsor

John Byrne who represents Allied Dunbar has Kindly sponsored this edition of the guide.

He believes that when it comes to financial planning, consumers today are looking for peace of mind and value for money.

John can offer trusted advice on the plans and services Allied Dunbar provides. Allied Dunbar are committed to ensuring that this is what they deliver to you, and as sponsors of The Essex Good Food Club Guide, hope you make the most of both.

Of course, any financial planning advice you decide to take will be in light of your own personal circumstances. We are not endorsing any of the plans or services on offer through Allied Dunbar.

The Essex Good Food Club

ALLIED DUNBAR

Professional advice for the life you don't yet know.

Restaurants

good food club guide

Establishments in this section are listed alphabetically in cuisine order.

Chili's

Cranes Park Road, Festival Leisure Park, Basildon, Essex
Tel: 01268 275678

Situated in Cranes Park Road at the busy Festival Leisure Park, this lively South-Western American restaurant proves to be extremely popular.
Originally founded in 1977 in Texas there are 5 privately owned outlets to date in the UK. Chili's certainly lives up to its reputation for providing first rate food and service that represents outstanding value for money. The large 204 seater air conditioned restaurant area benefits from a separate bar area that seats a further 40. The menu is crammed full of favourites such as tacos, quesadillas, burgers, fahitas, steaks, ribs, combos... and the portions are huge! The 'Guiltless Grill' section of the menu contains low fat healthier options for the health conscious and there is a good variety of vegetarian dishes to choose from. Children are very much welcomed and catered for at Chili's which makes this an ideal venue for families. A separate children's menu is available.

Opening Times: Mon-Sat 12-11pm Sun 12-10.30pm. Seats: 244. Average Price: £25. Private Parties: catered for. Car parking available. Vegetarian meals available. Children catered for. Air conditioned. Background music. Wheelchair access.

TGI Fridays

West Thurrock Way, West Thurrock, Grays &Unit 4 Festival Link, Festival Leisure Park, Basildon
Tel: 01708 861123 & 01268 534222

TGI Friday's has established itself as the premier American restaurant and bar. These lively venues famous for their elegant American 'clutter' adorning the walls are everything you would expect of a restaurant of this type... and more!
The now world famous menu offers a huge choice of dishes using authentic American ingredients where possible. Choose from burgers, steaks, skins, pasta, grills, salads, nachos, fahitas and more! Definitely worth a try is one of the dishes from the 'Jack Daniels Grill'. Portions are generous but for those with a smaller appetite there is plenty of choice including a variety of salads and sandwiches including an 'american Hot Chicken Sandwich' or 'Friday's Philly Steak Wrapper'. The choice of desserts is plentiful together with a number of larger items that are designed for sharing. Vegetarians are well catered for and dishes are clearly marked on the menu. A 'Sesame Street' menu is available for children. A separate bar area caters for those simply in search of liquid refreshments.

Opening Times: 7 days 12-11.30pm. Seats: 300 (Grays) 200 (Basildon). Average Price: £35. Credit cards:Mastercard/Amex/Visa/Switch. Private Parties: Any number. Car parking available. Vegetarian meals available. Children catered for. Air conditioned. Background music. Wheelchair access.

Aroma Oriental Restaurant

Festival Leisure Park, Festival Way, Basildon, SS14 3WB
Tel: 01268 527880

This recently opened, bright, lively and upbeat 'buffet' oriental restaurant enjoys a prime location on the busy Festival Lesiure Park in Basildon. There is a 260 seater resatuarant downstairs and an additional 100 seater a la carte restaurant upstairs which provides diners with a lovely view over the adjacent lakes. The 'all you can eat for a fixed price' menu includes a breathtaking selection of 80 dishes includingTepanyaki (japanese) dishes. From Monday to Friday lunch is £5.95 for adults and £3 for children under 11 years of age and £6.90 for adults on Saturday's and £3.50 for children. Sunday lunch times are slightly more expensive at £7.90 for adults and £4 for children. Dinner from Sunday to Thursday is £11.80 for adults and £6.80 for children. Friday to Saturday evenings there is a £12.80 charge for adults and £6.80 for children. A take-away service is available except on Friday and Saturday evenings (min order of £6.50).

Opening Times: Lunch Mon-Sat 12-3pm Sun 12-4pm. Dinner Mon-Fri 6-11.30pm. Sat 5.30-11.30pm. Sun 5-10.30pm. Seats: 260 (d/stairs) 100 (u/stairs). Private Parties: accepted. Car parking available. Vegetarian meals available. Children catered for. Background music. Air conditioned. Disabled facilities.

Chong's Restaurant

202 High Road, Loughton, Essex,
Tel: 020 8532 0442

This excellent Chinese restaurant was opened 8 years ago on the High Street in Loughton and has benefited from a tasteful refurbishment making it an even more attractive place to visit. The a la carte menu has been chosen with great care and brings together varieties from Peking, Szechuan and Canton ensuring that you are spoilt for choice. In addition to the a la carte menu, Chong's operate 2 'eat as much as you like' set menus: the 'Emperor' menu from Sunday to Thursday for £13.50 per person and the 'Deluxe Emperor' menu from Sunday to Friday priced at £15.50 per person (the costs are £7 and £8 respectively for children aged 10 and under). There are over 100 options to choose from and examples from the 'Deluxe Emperor' menu include mussels in black bean sauce, fillet steak Mandarin style or sizzling king prawns (main dishes). Chong's also operate an efficient take away service with a free delivery service (check terms and conditions). under the same management is Chong's at 170 Station Road, Chingford.

Opening Times: Lunch Mon-Sat 12-2pm Sun 12-11pm. Dinner Sun-Thurs 6-11pm Fri/Sat 6-11.30pm. Credit cards: accepted. Seats: 70. Average Price: £50. Private Parties: negotiable. Car parking available. Vegetarian meals available. Smart/casual dress. Children catered for. Background music. Air conditioned.

Dunmow's China Garden Restaurant

27 (1st Floor) High Street, Great Dunmow, Essex, CM6 1AB
Tel: 01371 872845 / 875298

Superb! Excellent! Wonderful! These are just a few of the adjectives used to describe this popular restaurant. Situated in the high Street at Great Dunmow, the experienced proprietor of 14 years is Kim Man whose clientele regularly wax lyrical about the wonderful cuisine on offer here! The opulent interior creates an authentic ambience where diners can enjoy a meal chosen from a truly sensational menu of over 130 quality Peking, Cantonese, Szechuan and Mongolian dishes. On the occasion of our correspondent's visit examples from the menu were deep fried crab claws stuffed with mashed prawn and crab, sliced beef with bamboo shoots and water chestnuts in oyster sauce and Mongolian hot pot lamb. Fish and seafood dishes are prominent and interesting options include grilled Dover Sole with ginger and spring onions in soya sauce, deep fried squid (Peking style) with sweet and sour sauce, and steamed Sea Bass with ginger and spring onions in soya sauce. A popular time is Sunday where a tremendous buffet is available at just £9.50 per person or £5 for children under twelve.

Opening Times: Lunch Tues-Thurs 12-2pm Sun 12.30-3pm. Dinner Mon-Sun 5.30-11.30pm. Seats: 100. Average Price: £30-45. Credit cards: Mastercard/Amex/Diners/Visa/Switch. Private Parties: Up to 100. Car parking nearby. Vegetarian meals available. Children catered for. Air conditioned. Background music.

The Gold Coast

202 Eastern Esplanade, Thorpe Bay, Southend-on-Sea, SS1 3AD
Tel: 01702 589388

Eastern Esplanade in Thorpe Bay provides the back drop for this large Chinese restaurant and entertainment venue. Opened two years ago, it has become increasingly popular amongst those who want to sample wonderful Chinese and Cantonese cuisines in more upbeat surroundings. Set out across two floors and enjoying a scenic view of the coast the comprehensive menu includes an extensive selection of appetizers, soups, seafood, poultry and beef and pork dishes. All dishes are reasonably priced with four set meals (for 2 or more persons) providing the ultimate feast. Variations range from £14 per person (vegetarian) to the 'seafood gourmet' at £25 per person (includes fresh lobster). The 'eat as much as you like' is £10.80 (lunch) and £13.80 (dinner). Entertainment at the weekend includes karaoke and live music making Gold Coast an ideal venue for private discos, dinner dances and other special occasions.

Opening Times: 7 days12-2pm & 6-11pm. Seats: 140. Average Price: £40. Credit cards: Mastercard/Diners/Visa/Switch. Private Parties: Up to 140. Car parking available. Vegetarian meals available. Children catered for. Air conditioned. Background music. Wheelchair access.

Joy Fook

Ongar Road, Kelvedon Hatch, Brentwood, Essex
Tel: 01277 372633 Fax: 01277 373056

Established 10 years ago and set in delightful countryside overlooking Bentley Golf Course (just north of Brentwood on the A128) is this elegant restaurant. The restaurant is traditionally decorated and has an intimate and cosy atmosphere and is perfect for enjoying the excellent cuisine. Popular with Frank Bruno and other celebrities, Joy Fook specialises in Cantonese and Pekingese cuisine. A full a la carte menu is available together with a choice of 6 set meals (including an English one). A good value 'eat as much as you like' buffet offering a staggering choice of dishes is available Sunday to Thursday 6pm-8pm (not available in December) . A live pianist provides background music on Tuesday and Thursday evenings whilst Friday and Saturday nights are disco nights. As well as being able to enjoy a meal in the restaurant, Joy Fook operates a take away service and benefits from a large private car park.

Opening Times: Lunch Mon-Sat 12-2.30pm; Sun 1-11.30pm. Dinner Mon-Thurs 6-11.30pm; Fri-Sat 6-12pm. Seats: 150. Average Price: £50. Private Parties: up to 150. Car parking available. Vegetarian meals available. Children catered for. Smart/casual dress. Background music/disco. Air conditioned. Wheelchair access.

The Cellar Bar and Bistro

4 Duke Street, Chelmsford, Essex
Tel: 01245 350353

Tucked away in the quaint alleyways in front of Chelmsford's cathedral is The Cellar - a great place to enjoy modern English cuisine.

Opened in 1983 and successfully run by Billy Brady, this small but lively bistro's charm is reflected in the beamed ceilings and soft gentle lighting. The bistro's menu offers a diversity of dishes providing light meals/snacks or a more formal style of eating. A 3 course set meal is available for just £9.95 offering good value for money.

This 26 seated establishment is available for private functions on Sunday's and would be a brilliant venue for celebrating a special occasion. An extensive wine list is available providing wines from around the world with prices starting from just £8.30 for a bottle of house wine. We suggest that booking is advisable to avoid disappointment as The Cellar can get very busy.

Opening Times: Food available lunch & dinner. Bistro Mon-Fri 7-10.30pm Sat 7-10.30pm. Seats: 26. Average Price: £33. Credit cards: Mastercard/Amex/Visa/Switch. Private Parties: negotiable. Car parking nearby. Vegetarian meals available.Air conditioned. Background music.

The Gables Restaurant

1 Fore Street, Old Harlow, Essex
Tel: 01279 427108 Fax: 01279 306524 www.gables.restaurant.co.uk

Situated in picturesque Old Harlow, this gem of a restaurant is housed in a delightful oak-framed building that dates back to 1460. With its wealth of original beams the Gables is full of old world charm! The current owners are Steve and Ann-Marie Taylor who have been in charge since 1991. The cuisine here is predominantly English although other influences are utilised to create impressive menus. The a la carte menu is comprehensive with an extensive selection of fresh fish (according to season), including popular favourites such as Sea Bass and Lobster. Examples of recent main courses include breast of duck, fillet of pork stilton and chicken with roast pepper sauce. Vegetarians are well catered for with examples such as aubergine lasagne or potato skins carbonara. Sweets are wide ranging including flambé dishes which are cooked at your table. Various table d'hoté menus represent excellent value for money, (for example 2 course lunch for £10). There is an impressive wine cellar with approximately 50 varieties from £10.25 for house to £39.50. An upstairs function room is ideal for parties up to 20.

Opening Times: Lunch Tues-Sat 12-2pm Sun 12.30-3pm Dinner Tues-Sat 7-9.30pm. Seats: 36. Average Price: £50. Private Parties: accepted. Car parking nearby. Vegetarian meals available. Children catered for. Background music. Wheelchair access.

the Cellar BAR & BISTRO

Situated in the quaint alleyways in front of Chelmsford's cathedral, the Cellar provides the highest quality of food and drink in pleasant and modern surroundings.

Opening hours

Bar: Monday - Friday 12.00 - 11.00pm
Saturday: 6.00pm - 11.00pm

Bistro: Monday - Friday 7.00 - 10.30pm
Saturday: 7.00 - 10.30pm

The Bistro menu offers a diversity of dishes, providing just light meals or a more formal style of eating. We offer an extensive wine list and a wide selection of bottled beers.

Table reservations: 01245 350353
No. 4 Duke Street, Chelmsford, Essex

The Gables

The Gables is the ideal venue for Luncheons, Dinners and Private Parties

Open

Tuesday - Saturday Lunch: 12 - 2.00pm
Dinner: 7.00pm - 9.30pm
Sunday: Lunch: 12.00 - 3.00pm

1 Fore Street, Old Harlow, Essex CM17 0AA
Telephone: 01279 427108
www.gablesrestaurant.co.uk

Little Hammonds
RESTAURANT

Fillet Steak with a Wild Mushroom Sauce (to serve 2)

Ingredients: 1lb of Wild Mushrooms (sliced and remove hard stalks)
1pt of good Beef Stock reduced to Glace of Stock

3 Shallots chopped finely
1/2pt of Double Cream
(2) 6oz Trimmed Fillet Steaks
1oz of Madeira

Method: Cook the Steaks as required and season.

Saute the Shallots until cooked but with no colour, add the mushrooms until they reduce down by half. Take out the mushrooms and then add the Medeira and reduce some more, add the beef stock and continue to reduce the liquor by half then add the cream and reduce by half again, add the mushrooms, season and nap over the steaks to serve.

White Chocolate Torte with Mint Choc Ice Cream

Ingredients: Sponge Base:
4oz Margarine
4oz Castor Sugar
4oz Egg
4oz Self Raising Flour

Method: Cream the margarine and caster sugar for 4mins on a medium speed, then scrape the mixture down, add the egg in a steady stream and then again scrape down, then add the flour with the mixer on a slow speed taking care not to over mix.

Bake at 170oc for approx. 15mins.

Mousse Filling: (1)1/2lb White Couverture Chocolate - heat to 60oc

1 Litre of Whipping Cream - Whip to double cream consistency
Add the heated chocolate quickly to the whipped cream and whisk until clear quickly or the mix will split. Put the sponge base in a 8 1/2 inch torte ring and pour in the chocolate mix to fill the ring. Leave to set.

Ganache: 11b White Ganache - Heat to 60oc
8oz Whipping Cream - Whip to double cream consistency
Add as the chocolate mousse. Pipe on to the top of the mousse

Little Hammonds

51 High Street, Ingatestone, Essex, CM4 0AT
Tel: 01277 355194

Established on its current site in 1987 by proprietor Stuart Hammond, this delightful restaurant continues to satisfy its numerous regular diners. The beauty of this 16th century building with its maze of rooms, low ceilings and exposed beams is the perfect setting in which to enjoy the excellent variety and quality of the food on offer. Examples from a recent a la carte menu included starters such as ravioli of scallops in a mussel and saffron broth, or warm smoked chicken on a herb and rocket risotto. Main courses could include saddle of venison with Anna and potato with blackberry and peppercorn jus. Extensive table d'hoté and set menus are always available including a 3 course meal including coffee for £25.50 per person. On Sunday's a special 3 course lunch is available at £12.95 per person. The wine list is extensive and includes more than 100 fine wines from around the world. Regular entertainment also features here and for those wishing to visit on a more regular basis there is a Little Hammond's 'gold card' which allows holders a 10% discount on meals, cigars & gift vouchers (cost of card for 6 months £20).

Opening Times: 7 days 12-2.30pm & 7-11pm. Seats: 80. Average Price: £45. Credit cards: Mastercard/Visa/Switch. Private Parties: Up to 65. Car parking nearby. Vegetarian meals available. Children catered for. Background music. Wheelchair access.

The Gallery Restaurant at The Chichester Hotel

Old London Road, Rawreth, Nr Wickford, Essex, SS11 8UE
Tel: 01268 560555 Fax: 01268 560580

Refurbished in 1999 and surrounded by open farm land is this family owned hotel in the village of Rawreth just off the A129. Run by David and Terry Harris, the beautiful Gallery restaurant is both quiet and comfortable creating a relaxing environment in which to enjoy the carefully prepared cuisine. An extensive a la carte menu is available during the week. In addition a table d'hoté menu changes weekly. A superb Sunday luncheon and dinner 'set price menu' is available at a reasonable price and all menus include complimentary coffee. The Stable bar at the Chichester with its wealth of old oak beams is a traditional English pub and serves a good selection of bar meals in the evening. The dinner-dance restaurant caters for up to 170 diners and dinner-dances are held regularly. The Olde Essex barn caters for up to 80 diners and is available for private functions such as weddings and business meetings etc. All 34 bedrooms have en-suite bathrooms. Some special tarrifs apply for those dining in the hotel restaurants

Opening Times: Lunch Mon-Fri 12.30-2pm Sun 12.30-2pm. Dinner 7 days 7-9.15pm . Seats: 60. Average Price: £50. Credit cards: Mastercard/Amex/ Visa/Switch. Car parking available. Vegetarian meals available. Music. Air conditioned. Wheelchair access.

Magic Mushroom

Barleylands Road, Billericay, Essex, CM11 2UD
Tel: 01268 289963

This 'interestingly' named restaurant was opened on its current site in October 1999 by proprietor and chef Darren Bennett. The modern British cuisine draws on many Mediterranean influences that help create a multitude of wonderful home made dishes. With a choice of approximately 10 starters, 10 mains and 7 desserts examples of recent dishes include sautéed kidneys in port, bacon, rosemary, sardine and fete mille feuille (olive and herb dressing) and wild mushroom and truffle soup (starters). Calf's liver with cassis sauce and garlic mash, wild boar with rich port sauce, poached pears and onion spatzle and roast cod with vegetables and truffle relish (mains). Typical desserts are creme brullé with fresh raspberries and chocolate marquis with cappuccino ice cream. A selection of European cheeses and home made chutney completes the experience. A further 2-3 daily specials are normally available. For wine lovers there is a selection of 64 varieties with most regions covered. For the more serious wine buffs there is a special 'connoisseur' selection consisting of 4 whites and 4 reds which are obtained by auction at Sotherby's.

Opening Times: Lunch Sun 12-3.30pm. Dinner Mon-Sat 6.30-10.30pm. Seats: 60. Average Price: £60. Credit cards: Mastercard/Visa/Switch. Private Parties: Up to 60. Car parking available. Vegetarian meals available. Smart/Casual dress. Children catered for. Air conditioned. Background music. Wheelchair access.

Milton Restaurant

61 Milton Road, Westcliff-on-Sea, Essex, SS0 7JP
Tel: 01702 313777

Situated in Milton Road, Westcliff-on-Sea and under the enthusiastic management of owners Sue and Andy this popular restaurant has built up a tremendous following and regular customers vouch for the delicious food that is always available here, together with the relaxing atmosphere and friendly service. In addition to the extensive menu crammed with delicious English and Continental dishes, diners have the opportunity of bringing their own alcoholic drinks (The Milton is one of the few unlicensed restaurants in the South-East). This actually benefits the customers as you do not have to pay high prices for drinks, therefore reducing the cost of a meal considerably! All food is reasonably priced and there is a special 3 course Sunday lunch available at £7.95 per person. It does get busy so it is advisable to book if possible!

Opening Times: Tues-Sat 6-10pm Sun 12-6pm. Seats: 28. Average Price: £20. Private Parties: up to 30. Credit Cards: Mastercard/Amex/Diners/Visa/Switch. Car parking available. Vegetarian meals available. Children catered for. Background music.

Milton Restaurant

Westcliff's Newest Bistro

Unlicensed - bring your own alcoholic drinks
Visit us and enjoy a wide range of quality English & Continental dishes, in a relaxing atmosphere.

All major cards accepted
Private parties welcome
Special 3 course Sunday Lunch £7.95

Opening Times
Tuesday - Saturday Eves: 6.00 - 10.00pm
Sundays: 12.00pm - 6.00pm

For further details
Telephone: 01702 313777
61 Milton Road, Westcliff

Mulberry Restaurant

Roslin
H·O·T·E·L
OVERLOOKING THE SEA

- Spacious restaurant & lounge with superb sea views
- Extensive menu
- Good value Sunday lunch
- Private car park
- All major credit cards accepted

Thorpe Esplanade, Thorpe Bay, Essex SS1 3BG Tel: 01702 586375 Fax: 01702 586663
www.roslin@aol.com

Mulberry Restaurant

Thorpe Esplanade, Thorpe Bay, Essex, SS1 3BG
Tel: 01702 586375

With an idyllic location on the seafront at Thorpe Bay, this attractive restaurant forms part of the Roslin Hotel. Guests can enjoy a meal whilst taking in one of the finest views of the Thames estuary. A family run business since the early 50's it enjoys a reputation for providing excellent food and service. The cuisine is a delightful mix of traditional English with many other European influences. All food is fresh and dishes are prepared to order. A full a la carte menu is available together with a range of additional daily specials. Typical examples of main courses could include grilled minted lamb steak, baked Trout, breaded escalope of veal or baked Swordfish steak. There is also an extensive bar menu with many additional options. The three course Sunday lunch represents good value at £11 per person and includes a choice of starters, mains and desserts. Children can select from their own separate menu making Mulberry and ideal venue for families.

Opening Times: Lunch Mon-Sun 12-2pm. Dinner Mon-Thurs 6.30-9.30pm Fri-Sat 6.30-10pm Sun 6.30-9pm. Average Price: £38. Credit cards: Mastercard/Amex/Diners/ Visa/Switch. Private Parties: accepted. Car parking available. Vegetarian meals available. Children catered for. Air conditioned. Background music. Wheelchair access. Accommodation.

Reeves Restaurant

Rumbles Cottage, Braintree, Essex
Tel: 0371 820996

Current proprietor/chef Darren Reeves opened this characterful restaurant in March 2000. The pretty village of Felsted is home to this attractive 16th century establishment which retains a plethora of original features. Set out across two floors, Reeves has three separate dining areas and guests can select from wide ranging a la carte and daily specials menus with al dishes being very reasonably priced. A la carte examples are smoked cheese rarebit, spiced prawn and avocado salad and griddled scallop and warm bacon salad (starters); and baked peppered salmon, cornfed chicken breast, grilled scotch sirloin or roast and confit duck (mains). To finish there are a range of desserts such as chocolate fudge cake, lemon meringue pie and home made fruit pie. In addition, there are special lunch menus including a 3 course Sunday lunch (choice of 5 starters, 5 mains and a selection of home made desserts) for £10.95. The wine list is ever increasing and will cover most regions.

Opening Times: Lunch 12-2.30pm Dinner 6.30-10pm. Seats: 48. Average Price: £50. Credit cards: Mastercard/Visa/Switch. Private Parties: catered for. Car parking available. Vegetarian meals available. Children catered for. Background music. Wheelchair access.

Riverside Restaurant

Old Road, Old Harlow, Essex, CM17 0HA
Tel: 01279 420985

We can certainly see why this fabulous restaurant is popular with the likes of Gary Lineker, Sol Campbell and Mike Read! Offering fine English cuisine with a difference and boasting an enviable position right on the edge of the river, this superb restaurant is the ideal place to relax and unwind. The menu changes seasonally and reflects all that is best in English cuisine. A typcial starter could be 'seared fresh king scallops served in a light and creamy curry sauce with toasted coconut' whilst a main course could be 'braised half leg of lamb stuffed with rosemary and garlic in a rich red wine sauce with braised vegetables'. In addition to the a la carte menu is a comprehensive specials board. The Riverside restaurant has a well stocked cellar incorporating a wide variety of wines and champagnes to ensure that whatever your choice of meal a suitable wine is available to accompany it. On Sunday lunch times you can enjoy a three course meal followed by coffee and mints for just £17.50. This venue is perfect for private parties (up to 150).

Opening Times: Lunch Tues-Fri 12-2.30pm Sun 12-4pm. Dinner Tues-Thurs 6-10pm Fri-Sat 6-11pm. Seats:120. Average Price: £60. Credit cards: Mastercard/Amex/Diners/Visa/Switch. Private Parties: Up to 150. Car parking available. Vegetarian meals available. Smart/casual dress. Children catered for. Air conditioned. Background music.

Russell's Restaurant

Bell Street, Gt Baddow, Chelmsford, Essex,CM2 7JR
Tel: 01245 478484 Fax: 01245 472705

Since taking over the running of this picturesque restaurant in 1991, experienced Barry Watson has been delighting the palates of discerning diners with a wide ranging menu consisting of modern English and continental dishes. Russell's is housed in a converted 14th century barn that oozes charm and character with its plethora of exposed beams. Typical of a la carte entrées could be mussels glazed with bacon, potato and parsley or artichoke heart with lobster in tomato and basil dressing. Main courses are suitably garnished and accompanied by a side order of vegetables and could include roasted partridge with goose liver and peach or Scotch fillet steak with 4 peppercorn and Brandy sauce. Fish dishes include Cod with chick peas, cinnamon, shallots and raisins or tiger prawns in champagne and lavender sauce. An excellent selection of desserts complete a meal perfectly. Various reasonably priced set menus are available and to accompany any meal there is an excellent wine list. Russell's is an ideal venue for weddings etc.

Opening Times: Lunch Tues-Fri 12-2pm, Sun 12-2.30pm; Dinner Mon-Fri 7-9.30pm, Sat 7-10pm. Seats: 80. Average Price: £68. Credit Cards: all major. Private Parties: up to 100 (150 for buffet). Car parking available. Vegetarian meals available. Children catered for. Background music. Air conditioned. Wheelchair access. Smart dress.

Fleur De Provence
Fleur De Provence
52
352987
Fleur De Provence offers pleasant surroundings in which to enjoy excellent cuisine, fine wines and unsurpassable standards of service.
Open for Lunch and Dinner
Bookings Welcome
52 Alexandra Street, Southend-on-Sea, Essex, SS1 1BJ
Tel: 01702 352987

Little Hammonds

51 High Street, Insatestone, Essex, CM4 0AT
Tel: 01277 355194

Established on its current site in 1987 by proprietor Stuart Hammond, this delightful restaurant continues to satisfy its numerous regular diners. The beauty of this 16th century building with its maze of rooms, low ceilings and exposed beams is the perfect setting in which to enjoy the excellent variety and quality of the food on offer. Examples from a recent a la carte menu included starters such as ravioli of scallops in a mussel and saffron broth, or warm smoked chicken on a herb and rocket risotto. Main courses could include saddle of venison with Anna and potato with blackberry and peppercorn jus. Extensive table d'hoté and set menus are always available including a 3 course meal including coffee for £25.50 per person. On Sunday's a special 3 course lunch is available at £12.95 per person. The wine list is extensive and includes more than 100 fine wines from around the world. Regular entertainment also features here and for those wishing to visit on a more regular basis there is a Little Hammond's 'gold card' which allows holders a 10% discount on meals, cigars & gift vouchers (cost of card for 6 months £20).

Opening Times: 7 days 12-2.30pm & 7-11pm. Seats: 80. Average Price: £45. Credit cards: Mastercard/Visa/Switch. Private Parties: Up to 65. Car parking nearby. Vegetarian meals available. Children catered for. Background music. Wheelchair access.

Paris Restaurant

7/9 London Road, Westcliff-on-Sea, Essex, SS0 9ST
Tel: 01702 344077

Situated on London Road, Westcliff-on-Sea, Paris restaurant was opened by current proprietor Wayne Hawkins in 1991. Since then it has built up a tremendous reputation as a first class restaurant and regular clientele travel from both near and far to sample the wonderful food on offer here. Wayne draws on the world's cuisine to develop his own unique style - this is not just a French restaurant! The interior is very stylish and creates a perfect atmosphere in which to savour dishes such as Squid with a honey and chilli dressing, beef fillet with rich red wine sauce, oriental duck, Sea Bass in pastry with chive sauce and asparagus. There is a delicious selection of desserts such as triple raspberry delight, peaches in a champagne soup and apple tart with blackberry ice cream (dishes are examples only as the menu is revised every few days). An extremely comprehensive wine list is available. Outside catering can also be arranged (with staff if required). Special events are a feature here and guests can be added to the regular mailing list.

Opening Times: Lunch 12.15-2pm and 7-10pm. Seats: 60. Average Price: £65. Credit cards: Mastercard/Amex/Visa/Switch. Private Parties: Up to 60. Car parking nearby. Vegetarian meals available. Children catered for. Air conditioned. Background music. Wheelchair access. Background music.

PARIS RESTAURANT
PARIS RESTAURANT
719 London Road,
Westcliff-on-Sea, Essex
Reservations:-
Tel/Fax: 01702 344077

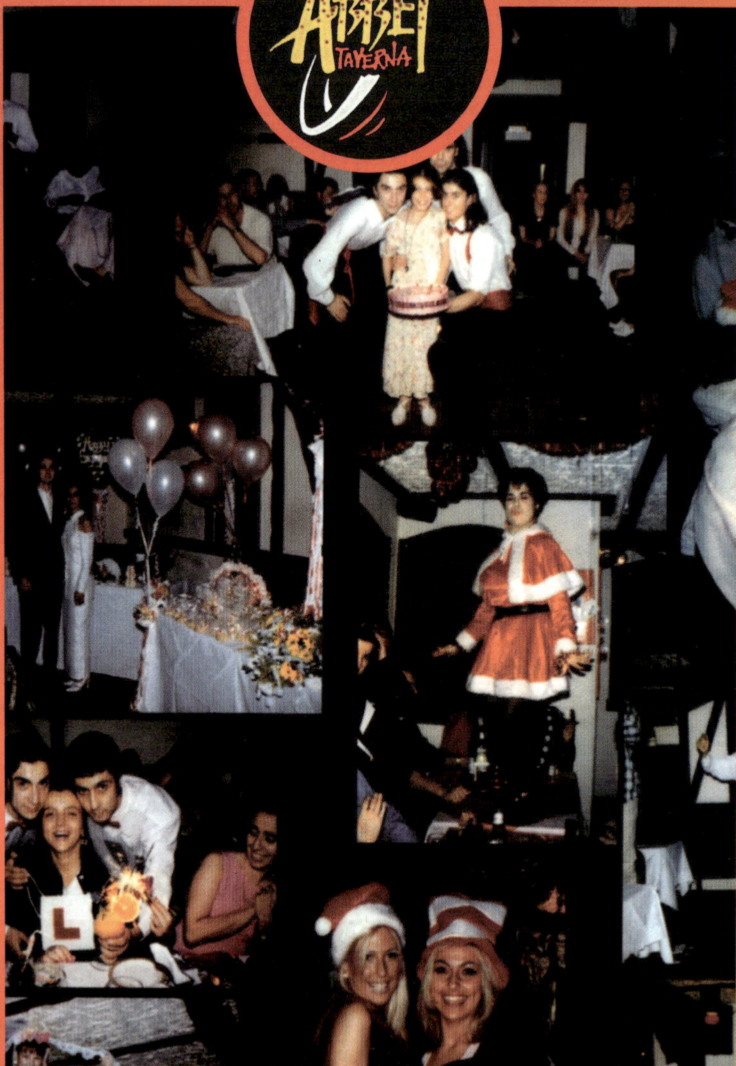

CAR PARKING

Parking is available nearby in Quakers Lane.

THE ABBEY TAVERNA

6 Foxes Parade, Sewardstone Road,
Waltham Abbey, Essex EN9 1PH
Telephone: 01992 767602 Fax: 01992 788566

Greek

Abbey Taverna

6 Foxes Parade, Sewardstone Road, Waltham Abbey, Essex, EN9 1PH
Tel: 01992 767602 Fax: 01992 788566

Established 12 years ago on its current site in Waltham Abbey, this 200 seat party orientated Greek restaurant specialises in providing excellent food, great hospitaility and a fantastic atmosphere. Occasions such as hen nights, birthdays, engagements and office parties are all catered for here 7 nights a week (booking essential).
Guests can select from a wide range of starters and main courses. Examples of main courses are kleftico, lamb cutlets, vegetarian lasagne or vegetarian pasta. Desserts include cheesecake, profiteroles and Tiramisu. The fixed price menu is £15 per person on Friday's or £24 with a half bottle of wine. Prices on Saturday are slightly more at £23 per person or £27 with a half bottle of wine. A Greek meze comprising of a variety of different Greek dishes including starters and main courses is also available (min 2 people). The good selection of wines and champagnes range from £10 (house) to £95 (Dom Perignon). As you would expect the entertainment includes traditional plate smashing and disco.

Opening Times: Mon-Thurs 8pm-1am Fri-Sat 8pm-2am. Seats: 200. Average Price: set price. Private Parties: up to 200. Car parking nearby. Vegetarian meals available. Smart/casual dress. Music. Air conditioned. Wheelchair access (with notice).

Indian

Akash

17 Laindon Centre, Basildon, Essex, SS15 5TE
Tel: 01268 546256 Fax: 01268 540082

Established on its current site over 20 year's ago, this popular Indian restaurant is situated in the heart of the Laindon shopping centre in Basildon. Diners can enjoy the excellent food here seven day's a week. The menu is comprehensive and all dishes are very reasonably priced. All the usual favourites are available but newly introduced exotic Balti dishes are proving very popular, originating from Baltistan which is situated on the border of Afghanistan and Pakistan. These dishes are richly spiced and include ground spices of coriander leaves, fenugreek and whole cumin. All the various options including chicken or lamb tikka, prawn, mixed vegetables and topical (mix) are served with nan (prices range from £5.95 (mixed vegetables) to £9.95 (topical). Other specials include the 'Akash special' (a complete meal for two) at £26 including dessert and coffee, and a two course set meal for two at £18.50. A take away service and free home delivery within a three mile radius is also available.

Opening Times: 7 days 12-2.30pm &6-11.30pm. Seats: 50. Average Price: £30. Credit cards: Accepted Private Parties: up to 50. Car parking Vegetarian meals available. Children catered for. Air conditioned. Background music. Wheelchair access.

AKASH

TANDOORI RESTAURANT AND TAKE-AWAY

FULLY LICENSED AIR CONDITIONED

FREE HOME DELIVERY SERVICE ON ORDERS **OVER £15** (3 MILE RADIUS) **7 DAYS A WEEK**

SPECIAL DISHES

A complete dish for two

Akash Special

(Served with starter, chicken tikka or sheek kebab, pulao rice, including dessert or coffee)

£26.00

SPECIAL BALTI DISHES

Newly introduced exotic Balti cuisine dishes originated from "Baltistan which is situated on the border of Afghanistan and Pakistan. Their style of cooking is completely different to that of other parts of the Indian continent. These dishes are richly spiced and served with a nan.

17 Laindon Centre, Basildon, Essex SS15 5TE

Tel: (01268) 546256 & 540082

Open 7 days a week including Bank Holidays

12.00pm - 2.30pm and 6.00pm-11.30pm

Except Friday - Closed Lunch, 6.00pm - 11.30 only

Raj Lodge

38 High Street, Old Harlow, Essex
Tel: 01279 626119

If excellent Indian food is your weakness, then this superb 80 seat establishment is an absolute must!! Situated in Old Harlow Raj Lodge has been tantalising local taste buds for over 12 years. Set out over 2 floors, the comprehensive menu contains a splendid selection of traditional Indian dishes combined with various more unique options such as 'hundi duck' or 'Pach mishali', (a mixture of chicken, lamb, venison, duck and king prawns).

Various set meals are extremely good value and include the Raj dinner at £26.95 for two persons. Sunday's are popular with a 10 dish buffet available at £6.95 per person.
Given its size, Raj Lodge is an ideal venue for party bookings (up to 50 in private room). All major credit cards are accepted. A take-away service is available with a 10% discount on take-away meals over £10 and 20% discount over £20 (collections only). A free home delivery service is also available. Ample car parking is available at rear of restaurant.

Opening Times: 7 days lunch & dinner. Seats: 80. Average Price: £35. Credit cards: All major cards. Private Parties: Up to 50. Car parking available. Vegetarian meals available. Children catered for. Air conditioned. Background music.

Raj Lodge

Tandoori Indian Restaurant

Fully Licensed & Fully Air Conditioned

Open daily

Lunch: 12.00-2.30pm

Dinner: 6.00-11.00pm

Free Home Delivery

Sunday Buffet £6.95 per person

10% Discount on Take-away meals over £10.00

20% Discount on take-away meals over £20.00 (on collections only)

We cater for parties

38 High Street, Old Harlow, Essex

Tel: 01279 626119

Shafique Bengal Blues Café Brasserie

30 The Green, Writtle, Chelmsford, CM1 3DU
Tel: 01245 422228 Fax: 01245 422569

Situated in the picturesque village of Writtle just outside Chelmsford, this imaginative establishment succeeds in combining traditional with contemporary. A grade II listed building is home to this most unique restaurant. The interior is a vibrant mix of bright decor and wooden floors that create an upbeat atmosphere where guests can enjoy a blend of traditional 'old time favourites' and more contemporary dishes. The menu is quite exhaustive and interesting dishes include 'sofyani bater' (tandoori skate, spiced with dry red chillies and fennel) or 'paneer rajshahi pasanda' (cottage cheese slices stuffed with spinach and served with almond sauce). Prices are very reasonable with main courses starting at £7.95. Special set meals are also very good value for money with lunch at £7.50 per person and Sunday buffet for £7.95 per person. This is not ;just a restaurant, several nights a week there is a resident DJ and diners are encouraged to utilise the purpose built dance floor! Ideal for parties, Bengal Blues Café is definitely a great place for those who enjoy a good night out!

Opening Times: Lunch Mon-Sat 11.30am-2pm & Sun 11.30am-11.30pm; Dinner Mon-Sat 5-11.30pm. Seats: 150. Average Price: £35. Credit Cards: most major cards Private Parties: up to 120. Car parking nearby. Vegetarian meals available. Children catered for. Background music/disco. Air conditioned. Wheelchair access.

The Shagor Tandoori

108 Hamlet Court Road, Westcliff on Sea, Essex,
Tel: 01702 347461

The enormous 94 seat Shagor Tandoori is situated in Hamlet Court Road, Westcliffe on Sea. The staff are friendly and attentive and the atmosphere convivial. The menu is exhaustive and reasonably priced. Highlights include special items such as the 'Three spices of Goa' which include a choice of 'jhinga caldeen' (king prawns cooked with spring onions, garlic, ginger, fresh green chilli and cream), 'chicken chacuti' (chicken cooked with special spices, green chilli, cashew nut and coriander) and 'lamb garam fry' (lamb cooked with special spices, vinegar,garlic and green chilli).Other chef's specials include king prawn dampoo, chicken tikka kalua kasta and peshwari chicken or lamb amongst others. The Sunday 'eat as much as you like' buffet is excellent value for money at £7.50 per person. Set meals (for four persons) are available including lamb (£60), chicken (£55) and fish (£75) - 24 hours notice is required.

Opening Times: 7 days 12-2.30pm & 6-12pm. Seats: 94. Average Price: £36. Credit cards: Mastercard/Amex/Visa/Switch. Private Parties: Up to 94. Car parking available. Vegetarian meals available. Children catered for. Smart/casual dress. Air conditioned. Background music.

Shafique
BENGAL
BLUES
CAFÉ BRASSERIE
A coffee bar atmosphere by day or a thriving dinning and drinking venue by night, soak up the atmosphere with the lavish bright modern decor, the mass of blazing colours, soft blues, jazz sounds and on Thursday, Friday & Saturday at 9.30pm....
...we turn up the volume.
30 The Green , Writtle, Chelmsford, Essex CM1 3DU
Telephone: 01245 422228 Fax: 01245 422569

Tandoori Parlour

61-63 Hart Road, Thundersley, South Benfleet, Essex
Tel: 01628 793786/793877

The Tandoori Parlour (the largest Indian in Essex) was opened in 1979 and over the years has established a reputation for exemplary Indian cuisine under the vastly experienced guidance of Mr Shah Ali. This modestly priced establishment offers an overwhelming choice for all lovers of Indian cuisine. A variety of 'specials' including 'Tandoori Kurchi Lobster' (24 hours notice required) will leave visitors spoilt for choice. One unusual appearance on the menu is Ostrich meat! In celebration of the 'Y2K' Indo-Bagla Food Festival, The Tandoori Parlour is holding a Sunday lunch buffet with over 50 tantalising dishes from different provinces of India and Bengal including Batak Masalla (duck), venison, king prawns, lamb and various vegetarian options. (children under 10 eat free!). With a large glass dance floor, laser lights and party atmosphere, this is an ideal venue for a special occasion. Disco's are held from Thursdays to Saturdays and occasionally cabaret acts such as Jimmy Jones, Mike Reed and Stan Boardman appear.

Opening Times: Lunch Mon-Sat 12-2.30pm Sun 12-12pm. Dinner Mon-Sat 5.30-12pm. Seats: 200. Average Price: £35. Credit cards: Mastercard/Amex/Diners/Visa/Switch. Private Parties: Up to 200. Car parking available. Vegetarian meals available. Children catered for. Air conditioned. Background music/disco. Wheelchair access.

Caffé Uno

275-277 High Rd, Loughton / 23 High St, Brentwood / 94a High St, Billericay
Tel: 020 8508 5399 & 01277 214111 & 01277 655789 www.caffeuno.co.uk

Although part of a group, each Caffé Uno retains its own individuality and is designed to suit its locality. The 3 outlets mentioned here are no exception. All have a modern Mediterranean look featuring terracotta tiles, natural materials and carefully chosen furniture. Imaginative wrought iron work plus an interesting mix of plates, bowls, pots and pictures create a modern vibrant and friendly atmosphere. the modern Italian menu features some classic pasta dishes: penne, spaghetti, lasagne and rich risottos. Every dish is freshly prepared to order, the sauces are all home made and the pasta served al dente. All pizzas are freshly baked and served with a choice of toppings drizzled with virgin olive oil and dressings with plump fresh olives. the list of 'specials' change weekly and children are given their own specially created menu with gifts and puzzles to take home. Caffé Uno is open seven days a week for breakfast, lunch and dinner.!

Opening Times: Mon-Sat 10am-11pm; Sun 11am-10pm Seats: approx 100. Average Price: £38. Credit cards:Mastercard/Amex/Diners/Visa/Switch. Private Parties: catered for. Car parking available. Vegetarian meals available. Children catered for. Air conditioned. Background music. Air conditioned. Wheelchair access.

Cantina D'oro

127 Broadway, Leigh-on-Sea, Essex, SS9 1PG
Tel: 01702 472187 www.cantina.sagehost.co.uk

This delightful Italian in Leigh-on-Sea is like a good wine.. it has improved with age! Established on its current sit way back in 1970, regular diners swear by its wonderful selection of classical Italian cuisine and fine wines. The service here is friendly and efficient and the a la carte menu and daily specials are a joy to behold. Various set meals are available and are fantastic value for money for just £11.50 (+10% service charge). A typical 3 course set meal includes a choice of approximately 6 starters (including items such as smoked fillet of mackerel and stuffed mushrooms Fiorentina). Amongst others, main courses could include grilled Dover Sole, steak Bordelaise and chicken Romana. Various desserts are served from the sweet trolley. An even more extensive Saturday night set menu is available at £14.50 plus 10% service charge. The wine list is comprehensive and compliments the food perfectly. Diners wishing to obtain more information can contact the restaurant's web-site on www.cantina.sagehost.co.uk.

Opening Times: Tues-Sun 6.15-10.30pm. Seats: 65. Average Price: £40-50. Credit cards: Mastercard/Visa/Switch. Private Parties: Up to 65. Car parking available. Vegetarian meals available. Children catered for. Smart/casual dress. Background music. Wheelchair access.

CAFFÉ UNO
The Original.
275-277 High Road,
Loughton, Essex
020 8508 5399
23 High Street,
Brentwood, Essex
01277 214111
94A High Street,
Billericay, Essex
01277 655789

Cosmopolitan Restaurant & Patisserie

8-10 Broomfield Road, Chelmsford, Essex
Tel: 01245 492020

If top quality Italian and continental cuisine is your weakness, then a visit to this charming restaurant is a definite must! Situated in Broomfield Road, Chelmsford and opened in 1999 the owner Franco Rusciani has utilised his vast experience in providing customers with a range of dishes that are sure to please even the most discerning palate.On the occasion of our correspondent's visit, the a la carte menu included starters such as 'fegatini fragrante' (duck and chicken liver, salad and garnish), 'duetto di mare' (grilled baby squid and king prawn on salad) and 'bigne' (savoury choux bun with cheese fondue and walnut sauce). Main courses included 'pesce spada' (fresh steak of swordfish), 'pollo al forno' (baked, marinated chicken) and 'mezza luna' (large home made ravioli with ricotta smoke salmon and spinach).A comprehensive vegetarian selection of starters and main courses are also available, as are numerous daily specials (vary).To compliment the food there is a wonderful wine list with many interesting wines from Italy and the rest of Europe.The Pattiserie on the ground floor is also worth a visit!

Opening Times: Mon-Sat 6-10.30pm. Seats: 70 (u/stairs); 40 (d/stairs). Average Price: £50. Credit cards: Mastercard/Amex/Diners/Visa/Switch. Private Parties: negotiable. Car parking nearby. Vegetarian meals available. Background music. Wheelchair access. Air conditioned. Wheelchair access d/stairs.

The Country Garden Restaurant

At The Good Intent, Crown Hill, Upshire, Essex, EN9 3SZ
Tel: 01992 769855

This charming Italian Restaurant was opened 14 years ago by Mario Pisanu and his wife Maria and forms part of the popular 'Good Intent' Public House. The separate 45 seat restaurant is on the 1st floor and is accessed by its own door. Mario's friendly disposition ensures that a visit here will be a memorable experience.The varied menu includes many celebrated dishes with meat, fish and pasta options well represented. Prices are very reasonable with hot and cold starters ranging from £3.50.The excellent meat selection include 'sizzlers' with your choice of meat served on a sizzling skillet. In addition the Sunday lunch menu is good value at £13.95 (3 courses) with a choice of six starters and six main courses. Downstairs 'The Good Intent' offers a comprehensive menu including a range of baguettes (baked to order) and nine pasta dishes.The wine list includes most regions with prices starting from £8.75 per bottle of house wine.

Opening Times: Lunch Tues-Sat 12-3pm & Sun 12-5pm. Dinner Tues-Sat 6-10.30pm. Seats: 45 restaurant, 50 pub. Credit cards: all major cards accepted. Average Price: £35. Private Parties: catered for. Car parking available. Vegetarian meals available. Smart/casual dress. Children catered for. Background music.

Flying Pasta

5/6 Shorefield Road, Westcliff-on-Sea, SS0 7RN
Tel: 01702 390250

Mr Domico has successfully run this very friendly restaurant for over 2 years now and has used all his experience and enthusiasm to provide diners with the 'true taste of Italy'. This brightly decorated 40 seater restaurant is set in a lovely position overlooking the sea in Shorefield Road and has a welcoming atmosphere. Selecting what you are going to eat may take a while as there are many delicious freshly prepared dishes to choose from. There is a good range of starters on the a la carte menu - a popular options is the 'antipasti amalfi' comprising of smoked salmon, prawn cocktail and avocados with seafood sauce. There are over 35 main courses including pizza, pasta, meat and fish dishes. One example is 'Bistecca campagnola' - sirloin steak cooked with mushrooms, peppers, onions, white wine, garlic and Italian herbs. The wall adorns 2 specials boards for even more choice. the wine list is just as extensive, the wines at flying pasta are imported directly so not only are they of excellent quality but they are cheaper too! Prices range from £8.50 for house wine up to £52.50.

Opening Times: Lunch Mon-Sat 12-2.30pm Sun 12pm-late. Dinner Mon-Sat 5pm-late. Seats: 65. Average Price: £50. Private Parties: accepted. Credit cards: Mastercard/ Amex/Visa/Switch. Car parking nearby. Vegetarian meals available. Wheelchair access.

Frankie & Benny's

Festival Leisure Park, Cranes Farm Road, Basildon
18 Southchurch Road, Southend-On_Sea
Tel: 01268 532522 & 01702 460732 www.frankieandbennys.com

This popular 1950's New York themed restaurant and bar has recently been awarded the prestigious 'investor in people' award. The friendly, relaxed atmosphere ensures that a visit here will certainly be a fun experience! The extensive menu is crammed with a mouth-watering selection of mid price New York Italian style offerings that can satisfy all the family. The main menu contains a mix of appetisers, side orders, pasta, pizza and house specialities. In addition, there are many special menus including an excellent 'value for money' lunch, where between 12-3pm (Monday-Friday), a 2 course meal is £5.95 or 3 course for £7.95 (not available on bank holidays). The size of Frankie & Benny's makes it an ideal venue for parties and there is a special party menu where groups of 10 or more can choose either a 2 course or 3 course meal for just £11.95 or £13.95 per person respectively. Children are welcome and can choose from their own 'gangster mice' menu (for just £3.95 for a 2 course meal including games and puzzles to keep them amuzed).

Opening Times: Basildon Mon-Sat 12-10.30pm Sun 12-10pm. Southend 7 days 9am-12pm. Seats: 157/150. Average Price: £30. Credit cards: Mastercard/Amex/Diners/Visa/Switch. Private Parties: catered for. Car parking available. Vegetarian meals available. Children catered for. Air conditioned. Background music. Wheelchair access.

La Bicicletta

37 Station Road, West Horndon, Essex
Tel: 01277 811697

This popular restaurant is owned by Albert Piras whose friendly disposition combined with the cuisine here ensures that your first visit to La Bicicletta certainly won't be your last! The variety on the menu is excellent and according to many favourable reports so is the food. In addition to the a la carte menu are severeal set menus offering great value for money and a daily specials board offering further choice. Examples of anitipasti (starters) include cozzee gratinate (mussels with herbs and spices gratinated with parmesan cheese) or carpaccio di manzo ruccola and parmigiano (thin slices of raw beef marinated with rocket and parmesan cheese). Main courses include petto di pollo alla Biciclette (breast of chicken in a champagne sauce garnished with courgettes) or spek and scamorza (smoked ham with scamozza cheese). There is a good range of Italian wines and beers to accompany your meal with house wine starting from £9.60.

Opening Times: Lunch Mon-Fri 12-2.30pm. Dinner Mon-Fri 6.30-10.30pm Sat 6.30-11pm. Seats: 60. Credit cards: most major credit cards accepted. Average Price: £60. Private Parties: up to 70. Car parking available. Vegetarian meals available. Children catered for. Background music. Wheelchair access.

There's a
F&Btastic!
Welcome at
Frankie & Benny's
NEW YORK ITALIAN RESTAURANT & BAR
BOOK NOW FOR CHRISTMAS
2 courses £12.95
3 courses £14.95
EXCITING RANGE
of American and Italian dishes cooked to Frankie and Benny's unique homestyle recipes in our open kitchen!
MAKE Frankie & Benny's a real night out with family and friends -
Great food!
Great bar! Great fun!
£3.95
All Inclusive Kids Menu with Games & Puzzles
Festival Leisure Park,
Cranes Farm Road, Basildon, Essex
Tel: 01268 532522
19 Southchurch Road, Southend-on-Sea, Essex
Tel: 01702 460732

Gerrardo's

23-25 Church Street, Great Baddow, Chelmsford, Essex, CM2 7HX
Tel: 01245 478884

Gerrardo's in Great Baddow is an excellent family run establishment that successfully combines a restaurant pizzeria and wine bar all under one roof!! The delightful premises enable diners to enjoy authentic Italian cuisine in traditional surroundings. The 110 seat restaurant boasts a comprehensive a la carte menu together with regular daily specials and set menus. The less formal pizzeria accommodates those wishing to partake of a mouth-watering selection of freshly baked pizzas, pastas and wonderful desserts. For those who just wish to pop in for a drink the wine bar offers a selection of wines, bottled (and draught) beers, spirits and cocktails. With regular live entertainment, Gerrardo's is an ideal venue for private parties. Gerrardo's also has its own Italian delicatessen and patisserie with many items not readily available in main food outlets. The delicatessen is situated at 157 Robin Way, Tile Kiln, Chelmsford.

Opening Times: lunch & dinner. Seats: 110 (restaurant) 30 (pizzeria). Average Price: £50. Credit cards: Mastercard/Amex/Diners/Visa/Switch. Private Parties: Up to 40. Car parking available. Vegetarian meals available. Children catered for. Air conditioned. Background & live music. Wheelchair access (pizzeria and wine bar only).

Grill Italia

258 High Road, Loughton, Essex, IG10 1RB
Tel: 0181 5088835

Opened in September 1999 and situated on the High Road in Loughton this quality Italian and continental restaurant has quickly established itself as an outstanding place to eat and drink.

The bright modern interior with wooden floors and large wall and ceiling mirrors creates an ambience that is light and airy. As well as pasta, chargrills and meat dishes, fresh seafood is much in evidence on the menu with additional daily specials offering further mouth-watering options. Examples at the time of our correspondent's visit (we understand that the menu is due to be revised) included chargrilled sardines or tomato and basil bruschetta (starters). Stuffed Monkfish tails with roasted red peppers, anchovies and saffron or veal chop on a mustard mash with port and wild mushroom sauce (main courses). To compliment, there is a well chosen selection of wines from different regions with prices from £9.95 (house).

Opening Times: Lunch Tues-Sun 12-2.30pm. Dinner Tues-Sat 6-10pm. Seats: 60. Average Price: £50. Credit cards: Mastercard/Visa/Switch. Private Parties: Up to 60. Car parking nearby. Vegetarian meals available. Children catered for. Air conditioned. Background music.

La Piccola Italia

Billericay Road, Herongate, Brentwood, Essex
Tel: 01277 811825

For those who do not speak Italian, the name of this delightful restaurant translates as 'Little Italy' and Aldo the genial proprietor (and chef) has seemingly transported a small corner of his home land to Brentwood! Situated adjacent to The Old Dog Inn at Herongate, the interior has recently been tastefully refurbished, including a number of hand painted murals. Visitors come from far afield to visit this friendly establishment and enjoy a meal in its intimate atmosphere. The main menu includes a wide range of starters, pastas, soups and meat dishes, all of which are reasonably priced, but the true strength of La Piccola is the superb range of fresh fish, with many various options including Sea Bass, Dover Sole, Lobster, Monkfish, Swordfish and Skate amongst the items that adorn the extensive daily specials boards. The extensive wine list is Italian, with a choice of 14 white and 14 red. La Piccola benefits from a large private car park.

Opening Times: Mon-Sat 12-2.30pm & 7-11.30pm. Seats: 55-60. Average Price: £50. Credit cards: Mastercard/Visa/Switch. Private Parties: Up to 70 (100 Sit down buffet). Car parking available. Vegetarian meals available. Children catered for (mid week only). Smart/casual dress. Background music. Wheelchair access.

Monty's Bar

1595 London Road, Leigh-on-Sea, Essex, SS9 2SG
Tel: 01702 712910

Fans of 'Cheers' will appreciate this extremely popular and lively venue run by Andrew and Claire Crow situated on London Road in Leigh-on-Sea. Opened in May 1995, recently extended and vibrantly decorated, Monty's offers an extensive choice of Italian dishes with Mediterranean influence - you really are spoilt for choice! All the dishes are freshly prepared, served up by friendly staff and offer great value for money. Examples from the menu include seafood crepes with Salmon, prawns and creamy herb sauce or Calamari fritti (starters). There are over 45 mouth-watering main courses and if that isn't enough there is a daily specials board offering a further 7 or so dishes. This restaurant has excellent facilities for parties with a purpose built dance floor (a DJ can be arranged on request). Monty's is also a great place for those in search of purely liquid refreshment. It has a well stocked bar serving a variety of beers and spirits.

Opening Times: Mon-Sat 12-12pm. Seats: 70 (120 for functions). Average Price: £40. Credit cards: Mastercard/Amex/Visa/Switch. Private Parties: up to 120 (sit down) 150 (buffets). Car parking nearby. Vegetarian meals available. Children catered for. Background music. Wheelchair access.

Papa Gino

24a Sun Street, Waltham Abbey, Essex, EN9 1EE
Tel: 01992 760915 Fax: 01992 714305

Expect a warm and friendly welcome from Gino and his genial staff at Papa Gino's situated on Sun Street in Waltham Abbey. Guests can 'dine and disco' until 1am in the first floor restaurant or for the more romantic at heart, you can dine downstairs to live background music (every night). Gino, the proprietor has been providing classic Italian cuisine here for over 13 years. A comprehensive a la carte menu is available and includes starters such as bread Brie served with a blackcurrant and port sauce. There is a vast selection of over 45 main courses to choose from including breast of Barbary duck in orange and Grand Marnier sauce or strongly recommended is one of Papa Gino's appetising specialities. The wine list is predominantly Italian and prices start from £8.75. There is a 'special cellar collection' with prices ranging from £22.95 to £69. Papa Gino can cater for weddings, business and private functions (up to 160) and set menus can be arranged from £17.95 to £25.65. Free car parking after 6pm is available nearby.

Opening Times: Lunch Mon-Fri 12-3pm. Dinner Mon-Sat 6.30pm-1am. Seats: 160. Creditcards: Mastercard/Amex/Diners/Visa/Switch. Average Price: £50. Private Parties: up to 160. Car parking nearby. Vegetarian meals available. Children catered for. Smart/casual dress. Background & live music. Air conditioned. Wheelchair access.

Piccolo

1-4 Shorefield Road, Westcliff on Sea, Essex
Tel: 01702 390370

For over 25 years this delightful restaurant has been satisfying the palates of discerning diners with its now legendary Italian cuisine. Situated on the sea front at Westcliff on Sea and enjoying a panoramic sea view, the walls are adorned with photos of many famous guests including Patsy Palmer, Freddie Starr and Jasper Carrot to name but a few! The menu is crammed with dishes embracing the flavours of the Mediterranean such as 'Cozze Marinara' or Northern Italian options such as 'chicken Valdostana' (with ham and mozzerella cheese, cooked in light white wine sauce). Fresh fish is a prominent feature with Skate, Sole, cutlets of Salmon and Shellfish being a sample of the locally caught varieties. Pizza and pasta dishes are very popular here with a mouth watering selection of both. Desserts could include Tiramisu, fresh fruits, profiteroles and a choice of dessert cheeses and Italian ice-creams and there are always a number of daily specials to compliment the a la carte selection. The wine list includes an extensive range of red, white and vintage reserve wines.

Opening Times: Mon-Sun 6pm-late. Seats: 55. Average Price: £35. Credit cards: Mastercard/Visa/Switch. Private Parties: up to 35. Car parking nearby. Vegetarian meals available. Children catered for. Background music. Air conditioned. Wheelchair access.

Deep Pan Pizza

33-37 Ripple Road, Barking & 102-106 South Street, Romford
Tel: 020 8594 0156 & 01708 732699

Following a total revamp of all its outlets, this popular pizza restaurant has become a firm favourite amongst customers searching for quality food, great value for money and excellent service. What Deep Pan Pizza have always done well, they now do even better! There is more here than just their famous freshly baked pizzas. Starters include 'nachos grande', meatballs el spicy, garlic mushrooms and the terrific value 'The ultimate combo' (including BBQ chicken wings, nachos grande, meatballs el spicy and garlic mushrooms, served with 2 slices of garlic bread with cheese). All this for 2 persons at just £9.99. Pasta specialities are all served with a slice of garlic bread and include; tagliatelle carbonara, lasagne al forno and penne vegetarian (pastas start from £5.29). The popular 'create your own' salad bar is £3.29 (as starter/side salad) or £5.50 (as a main course). The famous Deep Pan Pizzas come in 3 sizes, regular, medium and large and include amongst others 'The Green Grocer' (ham & mushroom), 'polynesian' (ham and pineapple), 'Catch of the Day' (Tuna, prawns, anchovies and sliced tomato). The restaurants are fully air conditioned and have full disabled facilities.

Opening Times: 7 days 12-11pm. Seats: 95/70. Average Price: £35. Credit cards: Mastercard/Amex/Diners/Visa/Switch. Private Parties: accepted. Car parking nearby. Vegetarian meals available. Air conditioned. Children's helpings. Wheelchair access.

Gerrardo's

23-25 Church Street, Great Baddow, Chelmsford, Essex, CM2 7HX
Tel: 01245 478884

Gerrardo's in Great Baddow is an excellent family run establishment that successfully combines a restaurant, pizzeria and wine bar all under one roof!! The delightful premises enable diners to enjoy authentic Italian cuisine in traditional surroundings. The 110 seat restaurant boasts a comprehensive a la carte menu together with regular daily specials and set menus. The less formal pizzeria accommodates those wishing to partake of a mouth-watering selection of freshly baked pizzas, pastas and wonderful desserts. For those who just wish to pop in for a drink the wine bar offers a selection of wines, bottled (and draught) beers, spirits and cocktails. With regular live entertainment, Gerrardo's is an ideal venue for private parties. Gerrardo's also has its own Italian delicatessen and patisserie with many items not readily available in main food outlets. The delicatessen is situated at 157 Robin Way, Tile Kiln, Chelmsford.

Opening Times: lunch & dinner Seats: 110 (restaurant) 30 (pizzeria). Average Price: £50. Credit cards: Mastercard/Amex/Diners/Visa/Switch. Private Parties: Up to 40. Car parking available. Vegetarian meals available. Children catered for. Air conditioned. Background & live music. Wheelchair access (wine bar and pizzeria only).

The Deep Pan Pizza Company
NEW MEGA PIZZA!
34 pieces only £14.99
Eat in or take-away
33 Ripple Road, Barking IG11 7NN
020 8594 0156
102-106 South Street, Romford RM1 1RX
01708 732 699

Piccolo

1-4 Shortfield Road, Westcliffe on Sea, Essex
Tel: 01702 390370

For over 25 years this delightful restaurant has been satisfying the palates of discerning diners with its now legendary Italian cuisine. Situated on the sea front at Westcliffe on Sea and enjoying a panoramic sea view, the walls are adorned with photos of many famous guests including Patsy Palmer, Freddie Starr and Jasper Carrot to name but a few! The menu is crammed with dishes embracing the flavours of the Mediterranean such as 'Cozze Marinara' to traditional Northern Italian options such as 'chicken Valdostana' (prepared with ham, mozzerella cheese and cooked in light white wine sauce).
Fresh fish is a prominent feature with Skate, Sole, cutlets of Salmon and Shellfish being a sample of the locally caught varieties. Pizza and pasta dishes are very popular here with a mouth-watering selection of both. The choice of desserts could include Tiramisu, fresh fruits, profiteroles and a choice of dessert cheeses and Italian ice-creams. In additional there are always a number of daily specials to compliment the a la carte selection. The wine list includes an extensive range of red, white and vintage reserve wines.

Opening Times: Mon-Sun 6pm-late. Seats: 55. Average Price: £25???. Private Parties: up to 35. Car parking nearby. Vegetarian meals available. Children catered for. Background music. Air conditioned. Wheelchair access.

Portuguese

Alvaro's Portugese Restaurant

32/34 St Helens Road, Westcliff-on-Sea, Essex
Tel: 01702 335840

1997 was a memorable year, the Queen's silver jubilee was a great cause for celebration across the UK. Amidst all the excitement, Freddy Alvaro took the opportunity of opening a rather splendid restaurant in Westcliff-on-Sea. Some 23 years later this popular Portugese establishment is still providing customers with a truly 'authentic' dining experience. Alvaro's is an immaculate restaurant where the provision of good food is taken very seriously. As you would expect seafood is always a prominent feature of the menu, although steaks, pork, poultry etc. are also well represented. Examples from recent menus include Portugese fish casserole, fillets of Sole in light egg batter and roast half duckling in port wine sauce. In addition to the a la carte selection there are numerous daily specials to choose from. The range of Portugese wines is excellent as are the various Portugese beers. Booking is advisable.

Opening Times: Lunch Tues-Fri Dinner Tues-Sun. Seats: 55-60. Average Price: £50. Credit cards: Mastercard/Visa/Switch. Car parking available. Vegetarian meals available. Children catered for. Smart/Casual dress preferred. Background music. Air conditioned.

EDELWEISS RESTAURANT
1613 London Road, Leigh-on-Sea, Essex
Telephone: (01702) 711517/521193
• Credit Cards Accepted
• Evenings & Mid-Week Specials
• Fully Licensed
• Parties & Weddings Catered For
• Established 1979
OPENING TIMES:
Monday to Saturday
Dinner from 7.00 p.m.
until 10.00 p.m. (last orders)
(Closed Sunday)
EDELWEISS RESTAURANT
Chef-Proprietor: Herbert Staudhammer

Edelweiss Swiss Restaurant

1613 London Road, Leigh-on-Sea, Essex, SS9 2SQ
Tel: 01702 711517

For the past 20 years chef patron Herbert Staudhammer has been successfully running this Swiss restaurant in Leigh-on-Sea. Drawing on his vast experience, herbert started his career in Zurich, moving onto Germany, Paris and then the prestigious German food centre in Knightsbridge. All these influences have enable him to create a range of mouth watering dishes that are prepared to order using only the freshest ingredients. Examples from recent menus include 'basler lummelbraten' (fillet steak larded with pork fat, roasted and sliced with kidney and served with roast potatoes, celery and cream sauce), or 'graubudner fleisch' (air cured beef served on wooden plate with black bread). In addition, there are many intersting specials which change daily. A three course 'schnitzel' menu is also available for £13.50 (Mon-Thurs only). Fondues are particularly popular. The sweet trolley provides ample choice and the extensive wine list (Swiss) compliments the cuisine perfectly.

Opening Times: Dinner Mon-Sat 7-10pm. Seats: 40. Average Price: £50. Credit cards: Mastercard/Amex/Visa/Switch. Private Parties: Up to 40. Car parking nearby. Vegetarian meals available. Air conditioned. Childrens helpings. Wheelchair access.

Turkish

Anatolians

104 Hamlet Court Road, Westcliff-on-Sea, Essex, SS0 7LP
Tel: 01702 390445

If you are in search of the ultimate night out including a mix of live entertainment and excellent food, then look no further than this vibrant 100 seat establishment in Westcliff-on-Sea. A good time is assured for small and large groups alike and guests can enjoy a wonderful range of mouth watering Turkish and international cuisine whilst enjoying the live music and exotic belly dancers.

The restaurant has been completely refurbished and the interior now provides an authentic, Mediterranean atmosphere which compliments the food and entertainment perfectly. At weekends Anatolians keep the party going until 1am. (This should ensure that some guests will definitely have a sore head the following morning!).

Opening Times: Dinner Mon-Thurs 5-12pm Fri-Sat 5pm-1am. Seats: 100. Average Price: £40. Credit cards: Mastercard/Amex/Visa/Switch. Private Parties: Up to 100. Car parking nearby. Vegetarian meals available. Children catered for. Smart/casual dress. live music/entertainment. Wheelchair access.

Other / Speciality

good food club guide

Establishments in this section are listed alphabetically and are non-specific cuisine.

Al Piatto

64 High Street, Brentwood, CM1 4AN
Tel: 01277 215522

Following a change in ownership and complete refurbishment, Al Piatto re-opened for business on Valentines night 2000. A good choice of evening considering the romantic nature of this quality Meditteranean restaurant! Set out across 2 levels the interior is a delightful mix of contemporary decor together with many of the building's original features including a wealth of beams.

Talented local chef Richard Young prepares a mouth watering array of innovative dishes to ensure visitors are not disappointed! On the occasion of our correspondent's visit, examples from the very reasonably priced evening menu included galia melon with orange fillets and gravelax of salmon (starters). Main courses included corn fed chicken breast with ginger and lemon, and whole Sea Bass with vanilla. The lunch time menu had a selection of 8 options including jacket potatoes with a variety of toppings, chef's special salad and a club-med sandwich. The well stocked wine list includes wines starting from £8.50 (house). There is also a downstairs bar for those in search of a drink!!

Opening Times: Lunch 11.30am-2.30pm. Dinner 7-12pm. Seats: 36. Average Price: £50. Private Parties: accepted. Credit cards: Mastercard/Visa/Switch. Private parties accepted Car parking nearby. Vegetarian meals available. Children catered for. Background music.

Bellini

1008 London road, Leigh-on-Sea, Essex
Tel: 01702 713996

Bellini is situated on the main London Road in Leigh-on-Sea. The tasteful interior of this modern bar/restaurant is a bright mix of vibrant colours, carpet, wood and tiled floors. The atmosphere in the separate restaurant area is very uplifting and on the occasion of our correspondent's visit the food was exceptional! The friendly staff are keen to please which makes a visit here even more pleasurable. The menu has a good range of starters, salads, pasta dishes, main courses and side orders. Examples include aromatic Quail, beef, lime and coconut spring rolls (starters), freshly prepared tagliatelle with a variety of choices, sirloin steak with shallot gravy and mash, baked chicken with chorizo sausage and watercress sauce (main courses). An excellent 3 course set meal including a choice of 4 starters, 4 mains and 4 sweets is available at just £9.95 (set party menus are also available). The wine list is extensive and covers most regions. A special 'Bellini' collection of wines range from £22.95 to £26.95.

Opening Times: Lunch Mon-Fri 12-3pm Sat-Sun 12-4pm. Dinner Mon-Sat 7-12pm. Seats: 65. Average Price: £45-50. Credit cards: Mastercard/Amex/Visa/Switch. Private parties: accepted Car parking available. Vegetarian meals available. Smart/Casual dress preferred. Children's helpings. Background music. Air conditioned.

Du Mauriers

New Street, Braintree, Essex
Tel: 01376 345615

This gem of a restaurant is situated just a stones throw away from the main town centre of Braintree. The restaurant is housed in a delightful 300 year old Grade II Listed Building and has been in the capable hands of proprietors David and Hilary Dukelow for just over a year. Set out across two levels the tasteful interior provides an intimate and relaxed atmosphere where guests can enjoy an eclectic mix of traditional and continental dishes that are all freshly prepared to order. The experienced manager, Dominique Mosconi, oversees the operation ensuring that a visit here will be an enjoyable experience. The chalk board menus change regularly and on the occasion of our correspondent's visit, examples included honey roast duck, medallions of pork and poached salmon. To compliment the excellent cuisine there is a comprehensive wine list incorporating varieties from most regions. During summer months there is a lovely patio area which is ideal for al fresco dining.

Opening Times: Lunch Tues-Sat 12-2.15pm. dinner Tues-Sat 7.30-9.30pm. Seats: 50. Average Price: £50. Credit cards: Mastercard/Visa/Switch. Private Parties: up to 50. Car parking available. Vegetarian meals available. Smart/casual dress. Wheelchair access.

Du Mauriers

- VARIED HIGH QUALITY CUISINE
- INTIMATE & RELAXING ATMOSPHERE
- EXTENSIVE WINE LIST

Du Mauriers

RESTAURANT

NEW STREET
BRAINTREE
ESSEX
TEL: 01376 345615
FAX: 01376 323443

Incognito

142 Sutton Road, Southend-on-Sea, Essex
Tel: 01702 464091

Romance is always in the air at this intimate (30 seat) establishment in Southend-on-Sea. Opened 5 years ago (on Valentine's night!), the chef/owner here is Mr Utz who has been catering for numerous love birds who enjoy not only their own company but also delicious freshly prepared international cuisine.
The menu is displayed on blackboards with a selection of approximately 6 starters and 6 to 8 main courses and 6 desserts, all of which change regularly. Even the names of dishes here reflect the romantic nature of the restaurant (e.g. 'when a man loves a woman' which is described as prawn and crab gently laid down on a crispy bed of lettuce and caressed all over with sauce Mary Rose!!!). A special 4 course candle lit dinner is excellent value at £16.95 (inc.). Open Tuesday to Saturday from 6.30pm 'til late, Incognito is a must for that more intimate occasion.

Opening Times: Tues-Sat 6.30pm-late. Seats: 30. Average Price: £38. Private Parties: up to 32. Creditcards: Mastercard/Visa. Car parking nearby. Vegetarian meals available. Children catered for. Background music. Wheelchair access.

Nick's Bistro

4 Station Road, Epping, Essex, CM16 3HA
Tel: 01992 575707

Regular visitors to Nick's Bistro in Station Road Epping, are familiar with the eclectic mix of fine cuisine and excellent wines that are on offer here. Proprietor Nick Philpott-Spruyt has established a friendly and attractive bistro where the provision of freshly prepared food has been the key to its success. The menus change regularly but examples of dishes available on the occasion of our correspondent's visit included starters such as deep fried Camembert with cranberry sauce and coronation chicken in lightly curried mayonnaise. Main courses included noisettes of lamb with port and redcurrent sauce and poached fillet of salmon with a lime dressing. There are various chalk boards containing approximately 10 further starters, 10 mains and a selection of mouth watering desserts. Another feature is the extensive selection of quality wines available. The bistro seats up to 60 in air conditioned comfort and there is a delightful patio which is ideal for Alfresco dining during summer months. Private functions can be catered for on request.

Opening Times: Lunch Mon-Sat 12-2pm. Dinner Mon-sat 6.30-10.30pm. Seats: 60. Average Price: £45. Private Parties: up to 60. Credit cards: Mastercard/Amex/Diners/ Visa/Switch. Car parking nearby. Vegetarian meals available. Smart/Casual dress. Background music. Air conditioned. Wheelchair access.

Rif-Raf's

101 Leigh Road, Leigh-on-Sea, Essex, SS9 1JL
Tel: 01702 482300

This informal bar/café in Leigh-on-Sea provides fresh food, great service and one additional benefit... it is totally smoke free!! Diners have certainly responded favourably to this brave move (booking at the weekend is definitely advisable). The very reasonably priced menu is a mix of many influences and combines a multitude of lighter options together with various dishes catering for those with larger appetites. On the occasion of our correspondent's visit, 'smaller things' included deep fried Whitebait, Thai fishcakes and crispy coated garlic mushrooms. 'Bigger things' included spaghetti with crab and bacon, chicken breast with lemon and Normandy pork with cream. Salads included avocado and prawn, chicken and bacon and Thai seafood. In addition there is normally a choice of approximately 6-10 daily specials (including fresh fish). The wine list is extensive and represents good value for money (house wine is £7.95 per bottle).

Opening Times: Mon-Thurs 11am-9pm & Fri-Sat 11am-10pm. Seats: 48. Average Price: £25. Credit cards: Mastercard/Amex/Diners/Visa/Switch. Private Parties: Up to 50. Car parking nearby. Vegetarian meals available. Children catered for. Background music. Wheelchair access.

Russell's Restaurant

Bell Street, Gt Baddow, Chelmsford, Essex,CM2 7JR
Tel: 01245 478484 Fax: 01245 472705

Since taking over the running of this picturesque restaurant in 1991, experienced Barry Watson has been delighting the palates of discerning diners with a wide ranging menu consisting of modern English and continental dishes. Russell's is housed in a converted 14th century barn that oozes charm and character with its plethora of exposed beams. Typical of a la carte entrées could be mussels glazed with bacon, potato and parsley or artichoke heart with lobster in tomato and basil dressing. Main course are suitably garnished and accompanied by a side order of vegetables and could include roasted partridge with goose liver and peach or Scotch fillet steak with 4 peppercorn and Brandy sauce. Fish dishes include Cod fillet with chick peas, cinnamon, shallots and raisins or tiger prawns in a champagne and lavender sauce. An excellent selection of desserts complete a meal perfectly. Various reasonably priced set menus are available and to accompany any meal there is an excellent wine list. Russell's is an ideal venue for weddings, catering for up to 150. An outside catering service is also available.

Opening Times: Lunch Tues-Fri 12-2pm, Sun 12-2.30pm; Dinner Mon-Fri 7-9.30pm, Sat 7-10pm. Seats: 80. Average Price: £60. Credit cards: All major cards accepted. Private Parties: up to 100 (150 for buffet). Car parking available. Vegetarian meals available. Children catered for. Background music. Air conditioned. Wheelchair access. Smart dress.

Smith's Brasserie

Fyfield Road, Ongar, Essex
Tel: 01277 365578

This trendy 100 seater establishment is located in Fyfield Road, Ongar and is renowned for its fresh seafood. Under the enthusiastic and experienced supervision of Alex the owner, this modern and contemporary restaurant truly provides a quality of food and service that is second to none. The fish lovers amongst you will be spoilt for choice. Starters include fresh crab and prawns with avocado and mayonnaise or 'fine de Claire' - a French variety of oysters. The choice of main courses is exhaustive but includes the likes of 'steamed Salmon with Hollandaise' or 'escallops of Monkfish'. Meat dishes are also available such as 'grilled chicken with mushrooms fried in lemon butter'. A superb 3 course set price lunch menu is available from Tuesday's to Saturday's and represents good value for money at £13.50. A carefully chosen wine list is available to compliment your choice of food which covers most regions. This restaurant benefits from a large car park.

Opening Times: Tues-Sat 12.30-4.30pm & 6.30-10.30pm. Seats: 100. Average Price: £55. Credit cards: Mastercard/Visa/Switch. Private Parties: Up to 25. Car parking available. Air conditioned. Smart/casual dress. Background music. Wheelchair access.

Webbers

2 Western Road, 11 High Street, Billericay, Essex, CM12 9DZ
Tel: 01277 656581 www.winecases.com

This excellent wine bar was established on its current Billericay site in 1976 by husband and wife team Brett and Gail Jones. The provision of top quality cosmopolitan cuisine together with a highly commended wine list assures visitors that a visit here will certainly be a pleasurable experience. The range of very reasonably priced dishes are all freshly prepared by Gail and can be selected from various printed and chalk board menus. Examples of recent offerings were starters such as melon with port and hot garlic bread with melted cheese. Main courses included baked potato stuffed with curried prawns, sirloin steak with tarragon butter and very, very hot chilli con carne. Mouth watering desserts included hot sticky toffee pudding and french apple flan. As a proud recipient of a prestigious wine diploma, Brett ensures there is always a tremendous selection of over 150 excellent wines covering all regions. Webbers also has its own wine club and from June 2000 a new internet based wine business will be up and running. For more information see Brett's new website at www.winecases.com.

Opening Times: Tues-Sat 12-2pm & 6.30-10pm. Seats: 65. Average Price: £30. Credit cards: All major cards accepted. Private Parties: up to 60. Car parking nearby. Vegetarian meals available. Background music. Air conditioned. Wheelchair access.

Pubs/Hotels

good food club guide

Establishments in this section are listed alphabetically.
(Cuisine's vary, see individual entries for details.)

The Bell

High Road, Horndon-on-The-Hill, Essex, SS17 8LD
Tel: 01375 642463 Fax: 01375 361611

Situated in the pretty and historic village of Horndon-on-the-Hill and certainly an inn not to be missed, is the Bell Inn, a privately owned establishment that dates back to the 15th century. The Bell provides excellent food, wine, spirits and beers along with good company in pleasing surroundings. A full menu is available in The Bell restaurant (also available in the bar area). The quality dishes using only fresh produce, have been recognised by the numerous awards they have received (including winner of Egon Ronay's "Pub chef of the year" 1993 and "Pub of the year" 1999 at the licensee industry awards). Examples from the menu include 'carrot and orange soup with duck tempura and maple' (starter), 'slow braised brisket of beef with girolles and oyster veloute' (main) and 'raspberry ice cream with a shot of champagne' (dessert). Fixed price menus are available with 2 courses priced at £15.95 or £17.95 for 3 courses. In addition to the menu is a huge specials board. Booking is an absolute must for the restaurant. Accommodation is also available at The Bell with room tariffs starting from £40 per night.

Opening Times: 7 days 12-1.45pm & 6.45-9.45pm. Seats: 36. Prviate parties: up to 36 seated, 50 buffet. Average Price: £50. Credit cards: Mastercard/Amex/Visa/Switch. Car parking available. Children's helpings. Vegetarian meals available. Background music.

The Belvedere

Hardings Elms Road, Crays Hill, Billericay, CM11 2UH
Tel: 01268 522828

This large food and entertainment venue is situated at Pipps Hill, Billericay just off the A127. The main feature here is the 7 day a week carvery which is available both lunch times and evenings at £5.95 per person. On Friday and Saturday evenings there are organised dinner dances. Friday evenings guests can enjoy a carvery and dance for £11.95 per person and on Saturday's there is an English/Continental menu comprising of approximately 8 starters, 14 main courses and 7 desserts. Guests can select their 3 options for £19.50 per person. The accompanying disco entertains the diners until 1am. Sunday lunch times are very popular at the Belvedere and guests can enjoy their lunch for £5.95 followed by varying entertainment including live jazz etc. Throughout the week there is always some form of entertainment including karaoke, live jazz and quiz nights. With 3 function rooms, the Belvedere is an ideal venue for private functions.

Opening Times: Lunch and dinner Mon-Sat. Seats: 150. Average Price: £35. Credit cards: Mastercard/Visa/Switch. Private Parties: accepted. Car parking available. Vegetarian meals available. Children catered for. Smart/casual dress. Music. Air conditioned. Wheelchair access.

The Black Lion

High Roding, Nr Great Dunmow, Essex, CM6 1NT
Tel: 01371 872847

Since taking over this charming 14th century coaching inn two and a half years ago, owners Brian and Fiona Day have built up an enviable number of regular satisfied customers! The welcoming interior with its unspoilt bar and beautifully decorated dining room creates ideal surroundings in which to partake of a relaxing meal. All the food here is organic and prepared to order using only the freshest of ingredients. Examples of recent main course include a superb chilli con carne, and a huge Dunmow gammon steak (including every conceivable extra!). Being an ex commercial fisherman, Brian has incorporated this knowledge in the breathtaking array of fish specialities including Barracuda, Lobster, Sea Bass, Black Bream and Red Snapper (there is upwards of 16 varieties daily). An extensive snack menu includes sandwiches, jackets and ploughman's. Desserts include an ever popular apple pie and 'home made' custard. Wine lovers can enjoy an excellent selection including a number of constantly changing 'bin ends' (red and white). The separate 'Rodings Bar' is ideal for families and children.

Opening Times:Lunch Mon-Fri 12-3pm Sat-Sun 12-late. Dinner Mon-Fri 7-9.30pm. Seats: 66. Average Price: £50. Private Parties: accepted. Car parking available. Vegetarian meals available. Children catered for. Background music.

... in Essex

BLUEBELL INN
Hempstead, Nr. Saffron Walden,
Essex CB10 2PD
Tel: 01799 599486

Tranquil setting belies the fact that the Bluebell was Dick Turpin's birthplace - the bar was once his butchers shop! 300 year old inn serves home prepared, traditional dishes. Sunday lunch a must.

THE CROWN
Stoke by Nayland, Nr. Colchester,
Essex CO6 4SE
Tel: 01206 262346

This 16th Century country coaching inn serves a traditional roast. Cask ales, good food and wines, cream teas are all available - perfect preparation for a walk along the Constable Trail. Large restaurant ideal for parties and functions.

THE DUCK INN
Newney Green, Writtle, Essex CM1 35F
Tel: 01245 421894

The perfect family inn. situated down a quite country lane, with children's adventure area. Bar meals and a full á la carte menu. Low beams and open fires; good ales and fine wines.

MARLBOROUGH HEAD HOTEL
Mill Lane, Dedham, Essex CO7 6DH
Tel: 01206 323250/323124

A charming 500 year old coaching inn in the heart of historic Dedham. Traditional bar serving cask ales and tasty bar meals whilst the restaurant has a varied á la carte menu and extensive wine list. Explore Constable Country from here. 3 letting rooms.

THE SUN HOTEL
High Street, Dedham, Essex
Tel: 01206 323351

Set in the heart of Constable Country, this beautiful Suffolk village house has been an inn for 500 years. It has a welcoming inglenook fireplace and a children's play area. The Sun serves bar meals, tempting daily specials and has an á la carte menu. CAMRA recommend the inn for the wide range of real ales.

For Business and Pleasure...

...we have the perfect location

Country Style Inns

COUNTRY STYLE INNS IS A DIVISION OF
Old English Inns PLC

Castle House, 21/23 Station Road,
New Barnet, Herts EN5 1PA

Telephone: 020 8275 3333
Fax: 020 8275 3334
www.oldenglish.co.uk

Bluebell Inn

Hempstead, Nr Saffron Walden, Essex, CB10 2PD
Tel: 01799 599486

The 300 year old Bluebell Inn at Hempstead near Saffron Walden is situated in a tranquil setting that very much belies the fact that the Bluebell was indeed Dick Turpin's birth place. The bar was once his butcher's shop!!
The 36 seat restaurant is non-smoking and creates the perfect atmosphere in which to enjoy a wide range of freshly prepared quality cuisine. All menus are displayed on blackboards with the main board displaying a choice of approximately 9 starters, 10 main courses (meat) and 6 fish specialities. Prices range from £6-£10.25 for a very large mixed grill. Other examples are pan fried chicken livers (starters) and chicken breast, marinated in Dijon mustard and lemon. A specials board is available with all items priced at £5. the desserts have their own board and include a choice of approximately 15 options. Children are provided with their own menu.

Opening Times: Lunch Tues-Sun 12-3pm. Dinner Mon-Sat 7-9pm. Seats: 36 (restaurant) 46 (bar). Credit cards: Most major cards accepted. Average Price: £44. Private Parties: catered for. Car parking available. Vegetarian meals available. Children catered for. Background music. Air conditioned. Wheelchair access.

The Bull (at Blackmore)

Church Street, Blackmore, Essex, CM4 0RN
Tel: 01277 821208

The Bull is a 14th century Public House situated off the beaten track in the pretty village of Blackmore near Ingatstone. Retaining a wealth or original features, it is a popular dining pub for those in search of quality food and comfortable surroundings. In addition to the main lounge there is a quaint 14 seat dining area (non smoking) that in a previous life formed the local bike shop! The menu includes many popular favourites including traditional home made pies, mixed grills and steaks. The daily specials include an average of 10 further main courses and there is a separate board featuring a number of fresh fish options. All dishes are prepared to order using only the finest local ingredients. Should you have enough room, it is worth trying one of the many home made desserts displayed on their own blackboard. Most regions are included on the impressive wine list (house wine £7.95). The bull does get busy so it is advisable to book. The lovely gardens are ideal for al fresco dining during Summer months.

Opening Times: Lunch Mon-Sat 12-2pm & Sun 12-2.30pm. Dinner Mon-Sat 7-9.30pm & Sun 7-9pm. Seats: 50 (smoking section) 14 (non-smoking section). Average Price: £28. Credit cards: Mastercard/Amex/Visa/Switch. Private Parties: catered for. Car parking available. Vegetarian meals available. Children catered for. Background music. Wheelchair access.

The Cherry Tree

Stambridge Road, Rochford, Essex, SS4 2AF
Tel: 01702 544426

This popular establishment is situated on Stambridge Road in Rochford. Open 7 days a week for lunch and dinner, a visit here is definitely worthwhile. Examples from recent menus include starters such as cheese filled tortollini, local, freshly smoked salmon, chilled melon and kiwi and marinated roll-mops. Main courses include options such as grilled duck breast, chargrilled salmon, wholetail breaded Scampi, mixed seafood pie with potato and cheese crust and fillet of lamb roasted with herbs. A wide range of desserts are available (according to season), and include home made pies and fresh fruit. In addition to the a la carte menu, other reasonably priced options include a choice of salads, ploughman's lunches and sandwiches. Extensive daily specials including starters and main courses are also available. It is worth keeping an eye out for various mid-week (Mon-thurs) offers, such as a 3 course special for £11.95 (inc. coffee).

Opening Times: 7 days 12-2pm & 7-9.30pm. Seats: 60-70. Average Price: £40-50. Credit cards: Mastercard/Visa/Switch. Private Parties: up to 40. Car parking available. Vegetarian meals available. Children catered for. Background music. Wheelchair access.

The Country Garden Restaurant

At The Good Intent, Crown Hill, Upshire, Essex, EN9 3SZ
Tel: 01992 769855

This charming Italian Restaurant was opened 14 years ago by Mario Pisanu and his wife Maria and forms part of the popular 'Good Intent' Public House. The separate 45 seat restaurant is on the 1st floor and is accessed by its own door. Mario's friendly disposition ensures that a visit here will be a memorable experience. The varied menu includes many celebrated dishes with meat, fish and pasta options well represented. Prices are very reasonable with hot and cold starters ranging from £3.50. The excellent meat selection include 'sizzlers' with your choice of meat served on a sizzling skillet. There are approximately 8 daily specials (starters and mains). In addition the Sunday lunch menu is good value at £13.95 (3 courses) with a choice of six starters and six main courses. Downstairs 'The Good Intent' offers a comprehensive menu including a range of baguettes (baked to order) and nine pasta dishes. The wine list is reasonably priced and includes most regions. Prices start from £8.75 per bottle of house wine, or £1.95 by the glass.

Opening Times: Lunch Tues-Sat 12-3pm & Sun 12-5pm. Dinner Tues-Sat 6-10.30pm. Seats: 45 restaurant, 50 pub. Average Price: £35. Credit cards: All major cards accepted. Private Parties: catered for. Car parking available. Vegetarian meals available. Smart/casual dress. Children catered for. Background music.

The Crown

Stoke by Nayland, Nr Colchester, Essex, CO6 4SE
Tel: 01206 262346

This delightful 16th century coaching inn is situated at Stoke By Nayland near Colchester, and a meal here would be perfect preparation for a walk along the Constable trail. Guests can choose to dine in either of the two restaurants here (one non-smoking). the main feature of this establishment is the wonderful carvery that was introduced in November 1999. Open from 12 to 9.30pm all day every day, the carvery provides a choice of roast at weekends and one roast during the week for a set price of £5.95 per person. All food is fresh which accounts from its popularity. There is an a la carte menu available in the evenings including a range of starters and main courses such as mixed grill, sirloin steak, fish and home made lasagne. A daily specials board also provides an alternative selection of dishes. Desserts are all home made. The Crown is ideal for families and there is a separate children's menu available at £3.50.

Opening Times: 7 days 12-9.30pm. Seats: 80. Average Price: £35. Credit cards: All major credit cards. Private Parties: accepted. Car parking available. Vegetarian meals available. Children catered for. Background music. Wheelchair access.

The Duck Inn

Newney Green, Writtle, Essex, CM1 3SF
Tel: 01245 421894

Tucked away down a quiet country lane, this is a perfect venue for those in search of top quality traditional fayre. The atmosphere is extremely welcoming with a plethora of low beams and open fires.

The menu changes regularly and examples of recent dishes included Whitebait, Brie wedges and king prawns (prices from £2.95). Main courses included plum duck, lamb cutlet, various steaks and aromatic duck (prices from £7.95). Fish is always prominent with Red Snapper, Salmon and Cod Mornay amongst the choices. The extensive vegetarian selection could include interesting options such as mushroom strogonoff or chestnut and mushroom parcel. Additional dishes are presented on the daily specials blackboard. The wine list is comprehensive and wines start at £8.95 for a bottle of house. Children are welcome and have their own menu.

Opening Times: Mon-Sat 12-2.30pm Sun 12-2pm. Dinner Mon-Sun 7-9.30pm. Seats: 70. Average Price: £34. Credit cards: Mastercard/Amex/Diners/Visa/Switch. Private Parties: catered for. Car parking available. Vegetarian meals available. Children catered for. Background music. Wheelchair access.

The Eagle

Ongar Road, Kelvedon Hatch, Brentwood, Essex, CM15 0AA
Tel: 01277 373472

The Eagle at Kelvedon Hatch is situated half way between Brentwood and Ongar. This cosy establishment has been run by Len Hands for 21 years during which time it has built up quite an enviable number of regular clientele.

The success lies in the fact that the wide range of traditional food on offer here is freshly prepared to the highest standard and is extremely good value for money. The main menu includes 14 starters, 25 main courses and 14 sweets. Thursday's at The Eagle are popular with quality fresh fish being delivered direct from Lowestoft. Items often include Crab, Dover Sole and even Lobster. Lunch time specials are available from Monday to Saturday at £4.25. A separate menu is available for vegetarians. A wonderful selection of freshly made desserts round off your meal perfectly. Sunday lunch is excellent value at £5.60 but be warned, the portions are huge!!! Although no children are allowed in the pub, there is a children's play area in the garden and is ideal for families during Summer months.

Opening Times: Lunch Mon-Sat 11-2pm Sun 12-7.30pm. Dinner Mon-Sat 6-10pm. Seats: 32. Average Price: £35-40. Credit cards: Mastercard/Diners/Visa/Switch. Private Parties: catered for. Car parking available. Vegetarian meals available. Children catered for. Background music. Wheelchair access.

The Foxhound

High Road, Orsett, Essex, Essex, RM16 3ER
Tel: 01375 891295

The Foxhound has stood on this site since 1893 although there has been a pub here since the 1600's. It has been run by the same family since 1961, with Jackie Firman having been at its helm for over 22 years. The building is very much unaltered, retaining a plethora of original features including the separate 'Fox's Den' Restaurant (est. 12 years) which was formerly The Old Coach House and Stables. Additionally the pub offers an extensive bar menu with many daily specials including a daily roast (except Sunday's). The Fox's Den is open Saturday and Sunday evenings and Sunday lunch (it is open on a bookable basis during the week). For a set price of £13.95 per person a three course meal is available and includes a choice of starters, main courses, sweets (or cheese & biscuits) & coffee. Sunday lunch is £8.95 (two course) and £4,75 for children. Regular celebration evenings in the pub are a highlight including St Patrick's Day etc. All menus reflect the theme and a six course dinner is £17. The Fox's Den is ideal for families (high chairs are available). NB. No credit cards accepted.

Opening Times: Pub Mon-Sat 12-2.30. Restaurant Sat 7-9.30pm & Sun 12.30-2.30pm. Seats: 40. Average Price: £35. Private Parties: up to 40. Car parking. Vegetarian meals available. Children catered for. Background music. Wheelchair access.

The Garnon Bushes

13 Coopersale Common, Epping, CM16 7QS
Tel: 01992 573096

The Garnon Bushes is situated at Coopersale Common, Epping on the former site of 4 railway cottages. The home made food here is predominantly traditional English and can be selected from an extensive and reasonably priced menu. Dishes include starters such as mushrooms with spicy dip, chicken liver paté and Scotch smoked salmon. Main courses include lamb cutlets, home made steak and kidney pie, corned beef hash and rack of lamb. There is also a choice of five fish dishes and four vegetarian options. Sweets include apple pie and cream, lemon cheesecake and creme brulée. Lighter bites include ploughman's, salads, sandwiches, baked potato and a 'great British fry-up'. The Sunday lunch menu has a choice of beef, lamb, chicken and pork for £6.95 (fish and vegetarian dishes are also available Sundays). There is a very good wine selection incorporating most regions. Children are catered for (main course £2.95) (sweet £1.50).

Opening Times: Mon-Sat 12-2.30pm & 6-10pm Sun 12-10pm. Average Price: £30-35. Credit cards: Mastercard/Amex/Visa/Switch. Private Parties: accepted. Car parking available. Vegetarian meals available. Children catered for. Background music.

The Green Man Pub & Restaurant

Naverstock Side, Brentwood, Essex, CM14 5SD
Tel: 01277 372231

This excellent pub and restaurant is situated at Naverstock side near Brentwood. The fayre on offer is a mix of traditional and international cuisines, that are all freshly prepared to order.

Proprietors Jan Bosdet and Bob Major have successfully run this attractive establishment for over 6 years and it continues to receive many excellent recommendations for both its food and its ambience. (During winter months there is an open fire creating a warm and welcoming atmosphere). The range of hot meals, cold smacks and sandwiches are available lunch times only and it is worth pointing out that Sunday's are becoming increasingly popular and guests are advised to book so as to avoid disappointment (Sunday lunch is £6.95 and is served from 12-3pm). There are also a selection of daily specials comprising of starters, main courses and desserts. There are a number of vegetarian options and children can also be catered for.

Opening Times: Lunch Mon-Sat 12-2pm Sun 12-3pm. Seats: 64. Average Price: £25. Credit cards: Mastercard/Visa/Switch. Private Parties: Up to 70. Car parking available. Vegetarian meals available. Children catered for. Background music. Wheelchair access.

The Green Man

Gosfield, Halstead, Essex
Tel: 01787 472746

It is not surprising that this picturesque 14th century public house has received a multitude of accolades including 'Essex Dining Pub of the Year' for the best traditional food in the county. Original beams add to the splendour of the interior. the hard working and courteous staff are led by experienced landlady Janet Harrington who has been here for 28 years. Janet together with daughter Rachel take immense pride in the preparation of freshly prepared (nothing is frozen) traditional English cuisine of the highest standard. all dishes are displayed on chalk boards and include a choice of approximately 16 starters and 18-20 main courses. Popular examples are home made steak and kidney pudding,pheasant in red wine (in season)and lamb chops in Port and cranberry sauce. The mouth-watering range of desserts are presented on a sweet trolley together with various cheeses. A small function room (30-40) is available for private functions and there is a very well kept garden.

Opening Times: Lunch 12-2pm. Dinner 6.45-9pm. Seats: 50. Average Price: £36. Private Parties: up to 40. Credit cards: Mastercard/Amex/Visa/Switch. Car parking available. Vegetarian meals available. Children catered for. Background music. Wheelchair access.

The Green Man

Toot Hill, Nr Epping, Essex
Tel: 01992 522255

According to many satisfied customers, the Green Man in Toot Hill is one of the county's best kept secrets! Open for food lunch times and evenings seven days a week, this romantic establishment dates back to 1907. Nowadays guests can enjoy the intimate surroundings of the 'courtyard' restaurant where a typical menu could include dishes such as stir fry oriental duck, cod and salmon terrine (starter), slowly baked lamb in garlic and oregano, pan-fried medallions of Monkfish, or breast of chicken filled with prawns and salmon mousse (main course). Overall, the delightful cuisine here is an imaginative mix of international cuisine and traditional English. A combination that deservedly won The Green Man a nomination for the prestigious Carlton London Restaurant Awards. Sunday lunch is very popular and it is advisable to arrive early. The wine list is first class, with a selection of wines to compliment any dish.

Opening Times: 7 days Lunch 12-2.30pm; Dinner 6-10pm. Seats: 80. Average Price: £20 (pub) 25 (courtyard). Credit cards: Mastercard/Amex/Visa/Diner/Switch. Private Parties: Up to 40. Car parking available. Vegetarian meals available. Children catered for. Smart/Casual dress. Air conditioned. Background music. Wheelchair access.

The Halfway House

Southend Arterial Road, Brentwood, Essex, CM13 3LL
Tel: 01277 811235

Situated on the main Southend Arterial Road at Brentwood, this food orientated establishment now has food available all day with early risers able to enjoy a hearty breakfast from 7.30am. Throughout the day there is a multitude of dishes available and at 6.30pm the main restaurant opens to provide a full a la carte selection of freshly prepared English and continental cuisine. In addition, an extensive range of daily specials including additional starters, main courses and desserts. All dishes are cooked to order. Sunday lunch is exceptional value for money, where for £8.95 you can enjoy a two course lunch chosen from 3 joints, fish dishes, vegetarian options and various other specials. Sunday lunch is available from 12-9pm and a selection of a la carte options plus additional specials are available on Sunday evenings.
During Summer months there is a marquee available for special occasions such as weddings etc. and can accommodate 150 guests.

Opening Times: 7 days. Seats: 80. Average Price: £40. Credit cards: Mastercard/Amex/Visa/Switch. Private Parties: Up to 60 (restaurant) 150 (marquee). Car parking available. Vegetarian meals available. Children catered for. Smart/casual dress. Background music. Wheelchair access.

Marlborough Head Hotel

Mill Lane, Dedham, Essex, CO7 6DH
Tel: 01206 323250

Marlborough Head Hotel is a charming 500 year old coaching inn situated in the heart of historic Dedham and is a perfect stop off point for those exploring 'Constable country'.
The varied a la carte menu incorporates many interesting options and examples of starters ranging from £2.95 include deep fried brie and highland salad. Main courses start from £7 and include dishes such as forest foul (double chicken fillet with a creamy wood mushroom sauce), knuckle of lamb in mint gravy and an 8oz fillet steak with stilton. Various desserts are displayed on their own blackboard (all £3.75). A daily specials board includes a further 4 starters and 6 main courses. A separate children's menu is also available. Three letting rooms are available - singles for £45, doubles for £55 and a four poster double for £65. All prices include breakfast and VAT.

Opening Times: Lunch Mon-Fri 12-2.30pm Sat-Sun 12-3pm. Dinner Mon-Sun 7-9.30pm. Seats: 85. Average Price: £35-40. Credit cards: Mastercard/Amex/Diners/ Visa/Switch. Private Parties: catered for. Car parking available. Vegetarian meals available. Children catered for. Background music. Wheelchair access.

Marygreen Manor

London Road, Brentwood, Essex, CM14 4NR
Tel: 01277 225252 Fax: 01277 262809 www.marygreenmanor.co.uk

This beautiful privately owned hotel and restaurant is situated just a stone's throw from junction 29 of the M25. Forming part of a delightful Tudor building, the interior of the 85 seat restaurant retains many original features providing wonderful surroundings in which to enjoy first class modern international cuisine. The extensive a la carte and fixed price menus draw on influences from Meditteranean to oriental together with many traditional options. Examples of recent a la carte dishes include a warm asparagus mousse with steamed asparagus tips and chervil butter sauce (starter) and pan fried fillet of venison fanned over a bramley apple & potato roesti with a compote of blackberries and glazed roast parsnips (main course). Desserts include hot banana soufflé served with toffee sauce or crepes suzette (for two). Various fixed priced menus include a three course meal (£26) and a three course Sunday lunch (£17.50). In addition, there is always a comprehensive snack menu available. The wine list includes a selection of over 200 fine wines from over 20 countries. A traditional cream tea is served in the afternoon (£5.15).

Opening Times: 7 days 12.30-2.15pm & 7.30-10.15pm. Seats: 80. Average Price: £80. Credit cards: Mastercard/Amex/Diners/Visa/Switch. Private Parties: on application. Car parking available. Vegetarian meals available. Children catered for. Smart dress. Air conditioned. Background music. Wheelchair access.

The Nags Head

Moreton, Nr Ongar, Essex
Tel: 01277 890239 Fax: 01277 890767

Viewers of the TV series 'Lovejoy' may recognise this pretty 16th century freehouse situated in Moreton with both the village and the pub being regularly used during filming. The current owner is Richard Keep and being a qualified chef, understandably places tremendous emphasis on the preparation and presentation of a wide range of freshly prepared traditional fayre, the quality of which would normally be found at top class restaurants! In addition to an extensive main menu there are approximately 10 additional daily specials including a mix of starters and main courses. A separate board includes a choice of 5 to 6 desserts. Sundays are popular and for £5.95 there is a choice of rib of beef, loin of pork, leg of lamb, steak and ale pie and home made toad in the hole. During Summer months there are BBQ's in the well kept garden. With a separate dining room The Nags Head is ideal for special occasions such as weddings etc. A kiddies menu is available with all dishes at £1.95 (including free ice cream).

Opening Times: Lunch Mon-Sat 11.30-3pm Sun 12-10.30pm. Dinner Mon-Sat 6-11pm. Seats: 50. Average Price: £48. Credit cards: Mastercard/Amex/Diners/Visa/Switch. Private Parties: In separate dining room. Car parking available. Vegetarian meals available. Children catered for. Background music.

The Plough Inn

Navestock Heath, Romford, Essex, RM4 1HD
Tel: 01277 372296

Navestock Heath is the pretty setting for this charming pub. The food is unashamedly traditional! The straightforward menu includes many tried and tested items which are all very much home made. In addition to the main lunch time and evening menus there are approximately four to five daily specials available which, on the occasion of our correspondent's visit included liver and bacon with mashed potato and peas (£3.75) and chicken or prawn curry with rice (£4.25). A favourite regular dish is the steak and ale pie. As with all the food here the desserts are also home made with the rhubarb or apple crumble being particularly popular. The Sunday menu always includes a roast of the day at £5.50 and additional dishes such as mushroom quiche (£3.95). Senior citizens are well catered for from Monday to Friday lunch times with an additional special menu. A separate function room is available for private functions and there is a large beer garden. A large car park is also available.

Opening Times: Lunch Mon-Sun 12-3pm; Dinner Tues-Sat 7-9.45pm. Seats: 60. Average Price: £20. Private Parties: accepted. Car parking available. Vegetarian meals available. Children catered for. Background music. Wheelchair access.

Rainbow and Dove

Hastingwood Common, Harlow, Essex, CM17 9JX
Tel: 01279 415419

Situated within half a mile of junction 7 of the M11 this characterful old public house was originally known as 'The Rainbow' during the time of Oliver Cromwell in the mid 17th century. Old photographs show that an ornamental bush in the shape of a dove once grew in the pub's forecourt (hence the addition to the name).The food here is wide ranging with various menus available lunch times and evenings, 7 days a week. The bar menu includes many good value house specialities. Hot and cold options including popular and unique house specialities such as rainbow brunch (jumbo Braughing sausage, bacon, mushrooms, tomatoes and potato dish, (Braughing being a place in Puckeridge, that provide these unique sausages). In addition, fresh fish always proves very popular as do the various dishes that make up the daily specials blackboard. The cosy little dining room can seat up to 18 and benefits from an extended supper licence (up to 12pm). A good wine list starts from £7.40 for house. Childrens meals are £1.95

Opening Times: Lunch Mon-Sun 12-2.30pm. Dinner Mon-Sat 7-9.30pm, Sun 7-9pm. Seats: 40. Average Price: £25. Credit cards: All major credit cards. Private Parties: Up to 18. Car parking available. Vegetarian meals available. Children catered for. Background Music.

The Rose & Crown

Ongar Road, Pilgrim's Hatch, Brentwood, Essex
Tel/Fax: 01277 372322

Standing in the ancient village of Pilgrim's Hatch, this delightful 15th century pub/restaurant has been run by Kim and Peppe Burelli for the last 15 years. Notable features of the interior include a huge brick fireplace, and original timbers still ornament the walls. The menu is crammed with many traditional dishes with a number of modern European options. Examples from recent a la carte menus include a fan of avocado and prawns and moules mariniere (starters). Main courses include king prawns in tomato, garlic and chilli sauce. In addition there is a daily specials board with a further choice of starters and main courses. A selection of home made desserts complete the experience. The extensive wine list includes most regions with special vintage wines available from £42 to £86. This pub is an ideal venue for private functions including wedding receptions. A corporate breakfast (min 20 persons) is available for busy executives at £15 per head.

Opening Times: Lunch Mon-Fri 12-2.30pm Sun 12-3.30pm. Dinner Mon-Fri 6- 10pm Sat 5.30-10.30pm Sun 6-10pm. Seats: 90. Average Price: £65-70. Credit cards all major cards. Private Parties: up to 90 (buffet 120). Car parking available. Vegetarian meals available. Smart/casual dress. Children catered for. Background music. Air conditioned. Wheelchair access.

The Sun Hotel

High Street, Dedham, Essex
Tel: 01206 323351

Set in the heart of Constable country, this beautiful village house has been an inn for 500 years. It's charming interior is enhanced by a welcoming inglenook fireplace. There is a separate non-smoking dining area where guests can enjoy a meal selected from a comprehensive a la carte menu. Examples of starters include paté, prawn cocktail and goats cheese (prices from £2.50). Main courses include beef bourginon, various steaks and grilled salmon steak (prices from £7.95). A choice of 4 pasta dishes are also available and a choice of 14 home made desserts include tempting options such as cheesecake, woodlands fruits and ice cream. Vegetarians are well catered for with dishes such as vegetable wellington (£6.25). Additional blackboards contain further daily specials and there is a special senior citizen's selection at £5.50 (main course and dessert). Children have their own menu and there is a separate family room to accommodate them. Four varying double rooms (all ensuite) are available (from £40 to £79.50 including breakfast).

Opening Times: Lunch Mon-Fri 12-2.30pm Sat-Sun 12.30-10pm. Dinner Mon-Fri 6.30-10.30pm. Seats: 40 (restaurant) 50 (bar). Average Price: £30. Credit cards: Mastercard/Amex/Visa/Switch. Private Parties: catered for. Car parking available. Vegetarian meals available. Children catered for. Accommodation.

The Waggon and Horses

Great Yeldham, Essex
Tel: 01787 237936

As you arrive at this delightful inn situated in Great Yeldham the first thing that catches your eye is the old horse drawn waggon which dates back to 1840. Formerly three 16th century cottages the building retains many of its original timbered features and has enjoyed a thriving trade since its current landlord Mike Shiffner took over in 1994.

The 32 seat restaurant area is ideal for those wishing to enjoy a truly home made meal in relative privacy. The menus are all on black boards with a selection of approximately 8 starters, 10 mains and 8 desserts. In addition a further daily specials board contains a further selection (currently priced at £4.95). Popular dishes include liver and bacon and the home made steak and kidney pie. Good value accommodation is also available at £15 per person including continental breakfast (full English £5 extra). A new extension is due for completion in September 2000 and will include a further 10 brand new rooms.

Opening Times: 7 days 12-2pm & 7-9pm. Seats: 32 (restaurant) 20 (bar). Average Price: £30. Credit cards: Mastercard/Amex/diners/Visa/Switch. Private Parties: up to 40. Car parking available. Vegetarian meals available. Children catered for. Background music. Wheelchair access.

The White Horse

39-41 Church Street, Sible Hedingham, CO9 3NT
Tel: 01787 460742

Dating back to the 14th century, The White Horse has immense character and atmosphere and many of its original features. The inn is said to be haunted and we understand that an exorcism takes place every 7 years. Regulars will almost certainly have noticed a marked improvement since Andrew and Helen McCracken took over in December 1999. Their expert management is no better illustrated than by the excellent variety of traditional home cooked food on offer. Diners can eat in the lounge or if preferred there is a separate (non-smoking) area that seats 20-24. There is a daily specials board as well as the main menu and the prices are very reasonable. This popular inn has a very large garden featuring a pond which overlooks open countryside. BBQ's are planned for the summer. Other various events take place including a monthly quiz night. The White Horse caters well for private parties including wedding receptions for up to 60 persons.

Opening Times: lunch Mon-Sat 12-2pm Sun 12-6pm. Dinner Mon-Thurs 6-9pm Fri-Sat 6-10pm. Seats: 35. Average Price: £35. Credit cards: Mastercard/Visa/Switch. Private Parties: up to 60. Car parking available. Vegetarian meals available. Children catered for. Background music.

Photographic Round-Up

The following pages contain a selection of establishments included in this guide.

Abbey Taverna
Waltham Abbey

Akash
Basildon

Alvaros
Westcliff-On-Sea

Anatolians
Westcliff-On-Sea

Aroma
Basildon

The Bluebell Inn
Saffron Walden

The Black Lion
High Roding

The Bull
Blackmore

Campanile
Basildon

The Cellar Bar & Bistro
Chelmsford

The Cherry Tree
Rochford

The Crown
Stoke by Nayland

The Country Garden
Upshire

Du Mauriers
Braintree

The Duck Inn
Writtle

The Eagle
Kelvedon Hatch

Edelweiss
Leigh-On-Sea

Fluer De Provence
Southend-On-Sea

Flying Pasta
Westcliff-On-Sea

Gables
Old Harlow

The Garnon Bushes
Epping

Gerrardo's
Great Baddow

The Green Man
Toot Hill

La Piccola Italia
Herongate

Little Hammonds
Ingatestone

Marlborough Head Hotel
Dedham

Marygreen Manor
Brentwood

Monty's Bar
Leigh-On-Sea

Nags Head
Moreton

Piccolo
Westcliff-On-Sea

The Rainbow & Dove
Hastingwood Common

Raj Lodge
Old Harlow

Reeves
Felsted

***Roslin Hotel** (inc. Mulberry Restaurant)*
Thorpe Bay

The Rose & Crown
Pilgrims Hatch

Russell's
Great Baddow

TGI Fridays
Basildon & West Thurrock

The Sun Hotel
Dedham

The Waggon & Horses
Great Yeldham

The White Horse
Sible Hedingham

THE
ESSEX
GOOD FOOD
CLUB GUIDE

How to Select the Perfect Wine

Wendy Lee of **Oasis Wines** offers some advice on selecting a suitable wine to accompany a meal.

There are several factors to consider when selecting a wine to go with the food you have chosen to enjoy in a restaurant. The days of white wine with chicken and fish, and red wine with beef are well and truly gone, thanks to creative cuisine and fusion dishes. For plain cooking the old principle still applies, however one is still faced with the dilemma of which grape variety would be the most complementary.

Ask the Waiter

The first and easiest way out of this quandary is to ask the wine waiter for his recommendation, but be sure to tell him your menu selection and the price that you are prepared to pay. This can however be a little embarrassing if you are on a budget and do not wish to advertise the fact to the company you are dining with. Furthermore, there are sadly on a few restaurants with trained wine waiters who can assist you professionally. Under this circumstance, the problem remains with yourself.

Food Analysis

It is important to look at your menu selection and analyse the ingredients that make the complete dish, together with the regional influence. Take for example Coq au vin - chicken cooked in red wine. A traditional French classic that harmonises best with a fine red burgundy. Nature assists greatly in wine selections and in most cases the origin of a dish will be complemented best by a wine from the same region. The 'white-wine-with-chicken' theory does not work in this case as the chicken has been cooked in red wine and so therefore the selection must be red - the same applies if the main ingredient is fish. If you make a steak selection, consider the sauce that accompanies it - in the case of pepper sauce, a full bodied red with peppery qualities on the palate is going to stand up to the pepper ingredient in the food and will linger well on the palate to result in a perfect marriage of the food and the wine. A Shiraz or Cotes du Rhone would be recommended in this instance. From this example we can also understand that we should select a wine which matches the weight of the dish; lightly cooked foods will harmonise best with light wines and hot foods with rich sauces will require a robust wine. Chinese, Thai and

Indian foods are far more complicated however, despite the common belief, I can assure you that lager is not the best choice! The correct wines work exceptionally well with all of these style of cuisine.

Food-Friendly Wines

It is probably worth memorising the following wines which will be 'safe' even if not the very best option. Whites: unoaked or lightly oaked Chardonney, Sauvignon Blanc and Pinot Grigio. Reds: Cabernet Sauvignon is a good 'food' wine, Merlot is an easy favourite and Pinot Noir can complement fish and light meals. Rose is under-rated but offers great versatility.

Food-Matched Wine Lists

As a specialist wine merchant to restaurants, Oasis Wines Ltd offers food-matched wine lists as a free service. Show this article to your favourite restaurants and allow us to help them to help you!.

Wendy Lee - Managing Director - Oasis Wines Ltd. Tel: 01702 394433

Popular Dishes Explained

Choosing from a menu can often be confusing when faced with the multitude of dishes on offer. To assist readers we have listed a number of popular dishes together with a brief explanation of each item. This, of course is not a comprehensive listing as differing cuisines, regional trends and chefs interpretations often result in variations but we hope it provides a useful guideline.

Starters

Foie gras - duck or goose liver, often made into paté
Gazpacho - a chilled Spanish soup of onion, tomato, pepper and cucumber.
Gravad Lax - raw salmon marinated in dill, pepper, salt and sugar
Guacamole - a creamy paste of avocado flavoured with coriander /and garlic
Hummus - a tangy paste of crushed chick peas flavoured with garlic and lemon
Meze - a variety of spiced Greek hors d'eouvre
Moules Mariniére - mussels in a sauce of white wines and onions.
Samosa - small pastry parcels of spiced meat or vegetables
Satay - small skewers of grilled meat served with a spicy peanut dip
Taramsalata - a creamy, pink paste of fish roe
Tzatziki - Yoghurt with cucumber and garlic
Vichyssoise - a thick, creamy leek and potato soup, served cold

Fish

Boullabaisse - chunky fish stew from the South of France
Coquilles St Jacques - Scallops
Lobster Newburg - with cream, stock and, sometimes, sherry
Lobster thermidor - served in theshell with a cream and mustard sauce, glazed in the oven
Sole Walewska - a rich dish of poached fish in a Mornay sauce with lobster
Sole bonne femme - cooked with stock, dry white wine, parsley and butter
Sole Véronique - poached in a wine sauce with grapes
Trout meuniére - floured, fried and topped with butter, parsley and lemon

Main Courses

Beef Stroganoff - strips of fillet steak sautéd and served in a sauce of wine and cream
Beef Wellington - beef in a pastry crust
Boeuf Bourguignon - steak braised in a red wine sauce with onions, bacon and mushrooms
Chicken a la king - pieces of chicken in a creamy sauce
Chicken Kiev - crumbed breast filled with herb butter, often garlic
Chicken Marengo - with tomato, white wine and garlic
Chicken Maryland - fried and served with bacon, corn fritters and fried banana
Osso Buco - Knuckle of veal cooked with white wine, tomato and onion
Pork Normandy - with cider, cream and Calvados
Ris de veau - calves sweetbreads
Saltimbocca alla Romana - veal topped with ham, cooked with sage and white wine
Steak au poivre - steak in a pepper and wine sauce
Steak bordelaise - steak in a red wine sauce with bone marrow
Steak Diane - steak in a peppered creamy sauce

Steak tartare - raw minced steak served with egg yolk
Tournedos Rossini - Fillet steak on a crouton, topped with foie gras and truffles
Wiener Schnitzel - escalope of veal, breadcrumbed and fried

Sauces

Aioli - strong garlic mayonnaise
Anglaise - thick white sauce of stock mixed with egg yolks, lemon and pepper
Arrabbiata - tomatoes, garlic and hot peppers
Béarnaise - thick sauce of egg yolks, vinegar, shallots, white wine and butter
Carbonara - bacon, egg and Parmesan cheese
Chasseur - mushrooms, tomatoes, shallots and white wine
Dijonnaise - cold sauce of eggs and mustard, similar to mayonnaise
Hollandaise - egg yolks and clarified butter
Mornay - creamy sauce of milk and egg yolks flavoured with Gruyére cheese
Pesto - basil, majoram, parsley, garlic, oil and Parmesan cheese
Pizzaiola - tomato, garlic, onion and white wine
Provencale - pepper and white wine with boiled egg whites, gherkins and mushrooms
Rémoulade - mayonnaise with mustard, capers, gherkins and herbs, served cold

Desserts

Banoffi Pie - with toffee and banana
Bavarois - cold custard with whipped cream and, usually, fruit
Creme brulée - caramel-topped, rich vanilla flavoured cream
Crepes Suzette - pancakes flavoured with orange or tangerine liqueur
Parfait - chilled dessert with fresh cream
Pavé - square shaped light sponge
Pavlova - meringue-based fruit dessert
Sabayon/zabaglione - Whisked egg yolks, wine and sugar
Syllabub - whisked cream, wineand sherry
Zuccott - a dome of liqueur-soaked sponge filled with fruit and cream
Zuppa Inglese - an Italian trifle

Culinary Terms

Coulis - a thin purée of cooked vegetables or fruit
Croustade - a case of pastry, bread or baked potato which can be filled
Devilled - seasoned and spicy, often with mustard or cayenne
Dim-sum - various Chinese savoury pastries and dumplings
Duxelles - stuffing of chopped mushrooms and shallots
En crouté - in a pastry or bread case
Farce - a delicate stuffing
Feuilleté - filled slice of puff pastry
Florentine - containing spinach
Goujons - thin strips of fish or chicken
Julienne - Cut into thin slices
Magret - a cut from the breast of a duck
Mille-Feuille - thin layers of filled puff pastry
Quenelles - spiced fish or meat balls
Roulade - stuffed and rolled
Sauté - to brown in oil
Tournedos - small slice of thick fillet

You've Bought The Book
Now Join The Club!

Free membership of The Essex Good Food Club is available to all purchasers of this guide. To join simply complete and return the form at the base of this page (no photocopies accepted!), and obtain the following benefits completely Free of Charge!!

Membership Benefits Include:

- Between Editions members will be informed of any changes in details relating to establishments featured in this guide, and receive regular updates including details of new openings etc.

- Details of Special discounts available to Club members at participating establishments.

- Advance notice of future editions and other Club publications.

To join complete this form and return to:
The membership secretary, The Essex Good Food Club,
P.O. Box 131 Berkhamsted, Herts HP4 3XT.

☐ I would like to join The Essex Good Food Club (Please tick)

Title (Mr/Mrs/Miss(delete as applicable)

Name ____________________

Address ____________________

____________ Postcode ________ Tel/FaxNo./e-mail ____________

Signed ____________ Date ____________

☐ (Please tick if applicable) **Additional Copies**

Please send me____further copies of the Essex Good Food Club Guide at £3.95 each (postage and packaging free). I enclose a cheque/postal order for £_____made payable to The Essex Good Food Club (including your name and address if different from above)

REPORT FORMS

The Essex Good Food Club welcomes readers comments on establishments both featured and not featured in this guide. Please complete the report form below (photocopies accepted), or just write to us, whichever is easiest.

Your comments, be them praise, recommendations or criticism, will assist in preparing future editions.

Return your completed forms to: The Editor, The Essex Good Food Club Guide, P.O. Box 131, Berkhamsted, Herts, HP4 3XT.

Name of Establishment: ______________________________

Address: ______________________________

Readers comments:

Readers Name: ______________________________

Address: ______________________________

Name of Establishment: ______________________________

Address: ______________________________

Readers comments:

Readers Name: ______________________________

Address: ______________________________

REPORT FORMS

The Essex Good Food Club welcomes readers comments on establishments both featured and not featured in this guide. Please complete the report form below (photocopies accepted), or just write to us, whichever is easiest.

Your comments, be them praise, recommendations or criticism, will assist in preparing future editions.

Return your completed forms to: The Editor, The Essex Good Food Club Guide, P.O. Box 131, Berkhamsted, Herts, HP4 3XT.

Name of Establishment: ______________________________

Address: ______________________________

Readers comments:

Readers Name: ______________________________

Address: ______________________________

Name of Establishment: ______________________________

Address: ______________________________

Readers comments:

Readers Name: ______________________________

Address: ______________________________

REPORT FORMS

The Essex Good Food Club welcomes readers comments on establishments both featured and not featured in this guide. Please complete the report form below (photocopies accepted), or just write to us, whichever is easiest.

Your comments, be them praise, recommendations or criticism, will assist in preparing future editions.

Return your completed forms to: The Editor, The Essex Good Food Club Guide, P.O. Box 131, Berkhamsted, Herts, HP4 3XT.

Name of Establishment: ______________________

Address: ______________________

Readers comments:

Readers Name: ______________________

Address: ______________________

Name of Establishment: ______________________

Address: ______________________

Readers comments:

Readers Name: ______________________

Address: ______________________

INDEX

INDEX

NOTES

NOTES

NOTES